A Man
Deprived

A MAN DEPRIVED

First published in hardback July 1993
by New Author Publications Ltd.

Second edition September 1994 Paperback
by The Publishing Corporation U.K. Ltd.

Haltgate House, Hullbridge Road,
South Woodham Ferrers, Chelmsford, Essex CM3 5NH.
Tel/Fax: 0245 320462.

Typeset: Red Planet Graphics, Romford, Essex
Tel: 0708 471718

Print: Redwood Books Ltd., Trowbridge, Wilts.
Tel: 0225 769979.

Cover Design: Joe Elgie.

Photographs: Kind permission
members of Mr. Lisner's family and friends.

ISBN 1 - 897780 - 85 - 0

The authors would like to thank

Rabbi Sober, retired now, and his successor, Rabbi Michael Harris, son of the Chief Rabbi of South Africa, for their help in the design of the sleeve of the book. Mary and Roy Miller for their unwavering patience and tolerance, and for the many cups of coffee and hours they spent helping to recall the events since 1971, and particularly Mary who edited so well the original text. Guy would also like to especially mention the staff at South Woodham Ferrers Library, who examined and criticised Volume I and helped to verify many of the dates and events of the Second World War. Larry, Maralyn and Suzanne, for the pain that they bore in relating their experiences and those of their dead sister, Estelle, and for recalling their childhood. Last but not least, Zelda of Wembley, who gave much needed advice and helped with the lead text. We thank you all.

DEDICATION

To all those who lost their lives under Nazi tyranny. Not just the Jewish people but all the others who fought against the evil that is Fascism. Most of all we dedicate this biography to the new generations who will carry the world forward, and especially to those who, even now, in many parts of Europe, think that nationalism, fascism, ethnic persecution and intolerance, because of a person's religion, colour or creed, is a credible pursuit.

Read this book, my young friends, and if but one of you changes your attitude to one of tolerance and understanding of your fellow man, then it has all been worthwhile.

Guy Nathan/Fiszel Lisner June 1993.

The book that you are about to read is true, bearing in mind that Fiszel is relating his story some 49 years after his release from Bergen-Belsen. The dates and facts have been thoroughly checked. Many of the details are as fresh as if they took place only yesterday. After reading this biography you may not look at life as you do now, ever again.

INTRODUCTION

The unofficial language of the Jewish people is Yiddish. It is a strange language, made up of mainly German words, bastardised by centuries of misuse and the spread of a nomadic people to all parts of the globe. How ironic that the common tongue, even more than the official 'Hebrew', is used as the means of international communication, and should have its roots in the language of those people whose past history is like an arrow in the heart of its users.

When Israel became an independent state in 1948, hordes of Jews scattered across Europe by the Holocaust, deprived of their homes and their families, made their way to the Promised Land. Yiddish was their common tongue, for they came from the 'Diaspora', the scattered tribes strewn across the continent. Those who were left alive and able.

From the far reaches of the Eastern provinces of Poland and Russia, from England and France and the Benelux Countries, from Asia, Iraq, from India, Ethiopia, Africa and the Empire of Great Britain, and from the United States of America, they turned towards their own country for salvation and the right to live in a free land, which had been denied them for too long.

Those over the age of 13 had been taught the traditional language, Hebrew, in the Sunday morning schools, the 'Heiders'. As soon as the two joyous days of celebration, shared with relatives and proud parents, were completed, they tended to forget their Hebrew teachings and reverted to the languages of their respective nations, and to Yiddish when they needed to converse with those of a different tongue.

Yiddish is the Jewish form of Esperanto!

Within the common language is the word 'Beshert'. This word often depicts the Jewish attitude to life. Fate. For that is what it means. 'Beshert' literally translated would be 'Que Sera Sera'. What will be, will be. If it is meant by God, by fate, by coincidence, then the Jew will say, it is 'Beshert'. It also has a hidden meaning of explanation, or non-explanation, depending on how you prefer to look at it.

When something occurs for which there is no logical explanation, then the excuse is, 'it is Beshert'.

When my wife and I strolled disinterestedly though the tiny South Woodham Ferrers market place on Thursday 17 December 1992, we had no inclination of what monumental event would be overtaking our lives. We also had no inclination to buy anything from the half-gloved, raw-faced traders who were defying the elements to earn their living, in spite of the economic recession which was prevalent in the U.K. at the time. While my wife idly gazed at a Christmas card stall, I wandered aimlessly among the stalls smiling, as is my wont when I'm feeling relaxed and I am about to have two of my novels published.

About halfway along the main passageway between the stalls I came upon one with an array of attractive looking ladies' garments hanging on rails around the edge of the stall, under a tarpaulin cover. My wife had asked me to take her to London to buy a new coat, and I was summing up the energy and enthusiasm that is needed to drive the horrendous journey to the capital, when I spotted exactly what I believed she was looking for. I wound my way back to the card stall and beckoned for her to come over. She purchased her usual assortment of cards and strode back with me to the clothing stall.

The elderly man with the soft eyes, the silver hair and lived-in face, short, stocky, smiling, approached us.

"Good afternoon. What can I show you?" he enquired.

He actually pronounced the 'W' in 'what', as a 'V', and I knew immediately that I was speaking to a 'foreigner'. His east European accent, which I had encountered many times in my early days in London's East End, and later when I travelled the world, immediately warmed me to the man. I smiled. He quickly returned his own smile. If he had been a woman I might have found myself attracted to him! He was sort of cuddly, and nice.

He engaged my wife in sales talk.

"Try the green one. It suits you, I can see already."

Petticoat Lane personified!

I allowed him to help her off with the one that she was wearing and on with his suggestion. It was too big. My wife is a little on the large side, but not yet an 18 or a 20!

"So, try the paler one, the avocado one on the rack over there."

Ah, the well-known convictions of ready approval he uttered. To my astonishment she liked it. Did you ever know a woman to like the second thing she tried on? I felt the time-honoured need to barter.

"How much is it?" I enquired.

"This one, let me see." As if he didn't know. "Should be £47.95, it's on the label."

"Hey, this is England and it's recession time," I countered.

Okay, already. The lovely lady looks so good in it, I'll do it for £45 only. I make a special price for you."

I smiled to myself. He was lovely, this little smiling east European Jew. So corny you could hug him!

I was about to give him a little more argument and continue the debate, when he said and did something that stopped me entirely in my tracks. All amusement disappeared.

"You say England? England? Thank God for England. Look what I got in Germany!"

I had seen it maybe once, twice before. I stood just a little flummoxed while fighting to keep the tears from welling up into my eyes. Jean saw it too. The sure sign of a concentration camp victim. The number 142097. The upside down triangle. Jean looked at me and I knew that the bartering was over. I wished I had never started it. He could have the full price and more if he needed it. It did not matter whether he was John Paul Getty, or living in a cardboard box, I only knew that I did not wish to cheat him out of one single penny.

I was going to buy the coat now anyway, even if my wife, as I expected, decided that she would not make her mind up immediately. But she knew! I wondered how all the people who had met this man reacted. Was he sick of the sympathetic tears? Was he fed up with people's immediate change of attitude?

I was just finishing my third novel T.O.E. It is a book about an Israeli spy and to write it I had investigated everything there was to know about Israel, the people and their first leader David Ben-Gurion. I knew that mark!

"Where did you get that?" I lamely enquired.

"I was in Auschwitz," he replied, somewhat less ebullient than he had been.

"Have you ever thought of writing about your experiences?"

"Thought about it, but never wanted to do it."

"Why? I know that to recall all the horrible experiences must be pretty traumatic for you, but don't you think it needs to be said?"

"Come away!" said Jean. She wandered down the market, rightly embarrassed by my enquiry.

"Many peoples have asked me. To be honest I have a story to tell like you never heard before. Even after I came to England I suffered incredible things."

He was about to tell me more, and did so, as I stood there listening, but I would not wish to pre-empt the story you are about to read.

Suffice to say that I cajoled him and pleaded with him, after telling him that I was a writer, and a little about my own traumas.

Okay. After 50 years I am going to tell. You really think I should?"

"Since Communism ceased in Russia and East Germany and the other countries, there has been a great rise in neo-Fascism and anti-Semitism once again. I think you owe it to the younger generation. In order to remind them. "LEST WE FORGET".

"The *Jewish Chronicle* and many others that I have met in this country and in Israel when I went there and even in America when I visited an old friend who survived with me, a lot of publishers and writers too, begged me to write. Never have I agreed. I like you. You seem very sincere and there is something about you. Okay. You write, I tell. How do we do it?"

I told him about the tape machine, and the many, many times we would need to meet. The enormous investigation I would need to do to verify and write his biography and to create a factual background so that the reader would be able to visualise those times. He smiled again.

T.O.E. could remain unfinished. I had only one task in my life now. Maybe our meeting was 'Beshert'?

The life story of Fiszel Lisner, Jewish Polish refugee, survivor extraordinaire is detailed in the following pages.

You will not gain pleasure from it. It is not a tale of fiction and imagined drama. It happened. It happened to this man.

You may stop and you may need to think.

I hope that after reading this incredible tale of one human being's personal suffering and lifelong tragedies, you will at the very least....feel.

CHAPTER 1

GERMANY 1918-1924

The decisions of important men retrospectively determine whether they are to be remembered with esteem. Mostly, they are innocuous and only seem to crave importance at the time of their making. Later, as years pass by, and the effect of apparently momentous decisions bear fruit, we decide on greatness, goodness and sometimes, notoriety. How then do we remember Herr Friedrich Ebert? Who, you may ask, is this man, for his place in history is not exactly surrounded with glory. When the Germans lost more than 750,000 of their sons, mainly at the Somme, during the final two years of the Great War, confidence in the Kaiser diminished to such an extent that Wilhelm saw fit to flee to Holland, and leave his country in its unholy mess. Quickly, the first Weimar Republic was formed as an unwelcome and involuntary amalgam of Christian and Social Democrats and Catholic Centre Parties. Their first President would be the man to end the war by suing for peace. Friedrich Ebert, the man who would make a rather horrendously catastrophic decision shortly afterwards, would be the one chosen to sit in a railway carriage in Versailles and agree to the harshest possible reparation agreement. It mattered not that Germany did not start the conflict originally. This was the ultimate responsibility of the Austrians and their enemy, the Serbs, who took it upon themselves to murder the Arch Duke Franz Ferdinand and his wife, while they were on a carriage ride through the streets of Sarajevo. Germany, who gave the Austrians all the support necessary, took the blame on their shoulders. The widely publicised reparation agreement angered the German people. It was clear that the country could not manage the hefty repayments without massive inflation, that must ultimately result in recession, unemployment and eventual depression.

The beaten soldiers returned to their homes, jobless and with their futures bleakly before them, for another aspect of the agreement of Versailles was to limit the armed forces to 100,000 men. With no money available for industrial investment, jobs were scarce and the whole country languished in the doldrums. To add to these problems, Ebert was forced to suppress a number of local uprisings where megalomaniacal little men of varying denominations and ideals claimed to form a new Government or asserted local territorial independence. It was the Communists in the south that were causing most of the problems, and so, with true management skills, he rallied a 'Free Force' of ex-servicemen to go to the illegal Communist Government headquarters in Munich and wipe them out. This they did, and with it, the usurpers' claim to be the true leaders of the divided country. That, however, was not the decision with which we are concerned. On the basis that the buck stops here, Ebert must bear the responsibility for creating a propaganda and intelligence department whose base would be Berlin, but whose centre of operations would be in Munich.

Appointed to this new unit was one, corporal Adolf Hitler, whose special responsibility it would be to investigate the Munich Workers Party. It was 1919.

History does not tell us whether Hitler pretended to inform his masters in Berlin on the activities of the MWP, or whether he actually did inform on them in the early days, or whether he fed the Weimar in the Reichstag a diatribe of stuff and nonsense. What we do know is that within a year Hitler had become the senior orator of that union, and within one further year its unopposed leader.

Whether the original ideology of the MWP could be labelled as Communism or Fascism is difficult to ascertain, as the policies of each were only separated by expansionist or nationalist doctrines within state control. Either way, Hitler saw the union set up as the vehicle for his widely nationalistic ideology, and as a source of personal sponsorship. As soon as he became its leader, he changed the name to the National Workers Party. In short, the Nazis! He formed a paramilitary section which was publicly labelled the stormtroopers, later called the S.S. The men who followed him came from the impoverished ex-servicemen who found a new beginning opening up for them, bathed in the sunshine of the extraordinary political colossus who was arising from the turmoil and the upheavals in Berlin. Ebert was little more than a figurehead, attempting continual appeasement of the three parties that loosely supported his presidency, while bowing to the demands of minority insurgents who continually questioned the correctness of his decisions and the validity of his position.

Meanwhile, our determined little corporal was gaining ever-increasing support from all sections of the community.

Hitler saw the need to appease the wealthy Aryan industrialists as well as the masses who flocked behind him in the belief that he was their saviour. His political rallies were widely reported, and in general, people across the land began believing that everything that was evil in the strife-torn country emanated from the Jews, Catholics, Blacks and non-Aryans.

In retrospect, as with all political leaders, some of his ideas were well founded and once implemented when he finally came to power, proved highly successful. Again in retrospect, it must be asked why he didn't court the Jewish wealth, power, influence and undoubted intelligence. Surely he would have risen to the chancellorship and

European domination more rapidly and with much less national and international uproar than that which eventually transpired. It is a question that is not answered in the annals of historical interpretation. We can only assume that his hatred of all things non-Aryan reigned high above his unquestionable desire to lead his country. For four years thereafter, Ebert struggled and Hitler rejoiced. His paramilitary organisation saw to it that no interference from the Communists and Jews accounted for much during demonstrations that invariably took place outside the halls and squares where he appeared to expound his extremist theories. By 1923 he mistakenly assumed that he had sufficient following to oust the Weimar Republic. News spread that at a mass meeting in Munich, Hitler was to declare a unilateral putsch. He would declare his Nazi party as the true government of Germany.

It was his first downfall. He had miscalculated the determination of the opposition. Outside the meeting hall, massive support for the democrats from every alternative section of opinion to those of the Nazis, rallied in their hordes. Inside the hall, people interrupted his speech and shouted their anger, vociferously disclaiming the usurper's pronouncements and predictions for the future of their country. Pandemonium ensued. The stormtroopers raised their rifles and people from all sides died in their hundreds. Hitler escaped with his life, but not before calm was restored and arrests made. Ebert, fearing further reprisal, levied a minor charge of insurgency and disturbing the peace against Hitler and he was jailed for ten months.

Would that Ebert had elected some other nominee to carry out the investigation into the MWP! Would that Ebert had charged Hitler with the true crimes that he had committed! What would history have recorded? How many people would be alive today? How many

Jews would not have perished in the death camps under the evil tyrant that emerged after that extraordinarily lenient sentence. The Nazis temporarily disbanded. It was during his time spent in moderate luxury, as many of the prison guards were his supporters, that Hitler wrote the book that expounded his dreams and ideas, and what he regarded as his struggles, *Mein Kampf.* Getting it published was no problem, and though he emerged in January 1924 to a beaten and disillusioned party of disgraced former supporters, his popularity spread and he became somewhat of a national hero.

The writer has not established the exact date of his release, but it would seem to be at the beginning of January.

The date, January 1924, is peculiarly and coincidentally significant, because it was on the second of that same month, in the same year, that Estera-Laja Lisner, nee Kaszewicz, lay in her bed of downy chicken feathers most painfully bearing down on her swollen abdomen, in order to give life to her first child, the boy Fiszel.

She had been married with the approval of her father, a rabbi, to Luzer Lisner, some two years previously.

CHAPTER 2

EUROPE 1924-1939

'First, their synagogues should be set on fire, and whatever does not burn should be covered or spread over with dirt so that no one may ever be able to see a cinder or stone of it. Jewish homes should likewise be broken down or destroyed.

The Jews should then be put under one roof, or a stable, like gypsies, in order that they may realise that they are not masters in our land. They should be put to work, to earn their living, by the sweat of their noses, and even then, if they are regarded as too dangerous, these poisonous bitter worms should be stripped of their belongings, which they have extorted usuriously from us, and driven out of the country for all time.'

You may believe that these are the words of the Nazi tyrant, Adolf Hitler. In fact they were written in 1543 by Martin Luther. Is it then any wonder that a resurgence of such hatred should occur in the twentieth century? Can we believe that there will never again be a man filled with hatred, an opportunity seeker, a man skilled in recognising the weaknesses of his nation. A man to rally support for vengeance on the accidental religious birth of one people.

Throughout history nations have followed, in various degrees, the doctrines and advice of Martin Luther.

England, France, Spain, Portugal, Bohemia, Italy and Zsarist Russia are among the nations that have, from time to time, inflicted their own inadequacy upon the most victimised and suppressed people in the world. Can it really be that Christianity truly blames the entire race for the death of The Son of God? Even with the enormous following that Jesus has invoked, it is beyond belief that revenge

7

in the form of an everlasting vendetta could be harboured for 2,000 years. And yet, as I write, there is an upsurge of neo-fascism in Europe with the denunciation of the eastern bloc style of Communism.

The suburb of Zdunska-Wola known as Ulicia-Szrazka, number 28, in the region of Szeracz, was one of many that was regarded as exclusively Jewish in the town. It was not the poorest, but languished near the bottom of the wealth league, inhabited as it was by those who generally enjoyed regular employment, albeit of a lowly regard. The Szeraczians were not the mill owners, or shopkeepers or managers of the many clothing and material producers. More, they were the workers who manned the machines from dawn to dusk on low pay, in uncompromising conditions. Except for a few, who chose to earn their living by other means, and who had parents or grandparents who were the owners of small firms. One among these was Luzer Lisner. He had chosen to gain a living as a self-employed interior decorator.

It was not a trade that many who enjoyed youthful wisdom would have chosen for a young man, for it was impossible to carry out many of the requirements in the long freezing winter months. The bitter mid-eastern European conditions, when the temperature would drop to as low as 20 degrees below freezing point, restricted the desire of Luzer to earn his living independently. Even though he owned his own house, a two-storey, two-up and two-down stone and concrete terrace set in a long line of similarly constructed establishments, he was never to enjoy the benefits of self-employment. As is the Jewish way, he lived by guile and effort and a little help from his wife's family and from his father, who owned a kosher butcher shop close by. During the long hard winter days, when no one required decoration or alteration to their properties,

Luzer could be seen setting off for the cattle markets in Lodz, 60 kilometres away, to purchase live stock for the shop. With an extra mouth to feed, his yearning for an independent life-style that earned the envy of his fellow Jews, would have to be compromised in favour of the need to keep the wolf from the door. Proudly he called his friends together to show them his new born son, a fine sturdy boy who would achieve more than he ever could. It is the dream of all Jews everywhere, for they do not believe in reincarnation, but only in making the world a better place for their dependants.

At the 'Briss', traditionally eight days after the birth, he exclaimed his joy to his many friends, all who dwelt among the ramshackle buildings that was Ulicia-Szerazka.

Luzer was 27 years old and his young beautiful wife, Estera-Laja, just 20. Little did they know of the future, or even the present. There were no cat's whisker. They could not afford or even read any of the daily journals or newspapers, except for the in-house Jewish magazine that the schul printed once a month. Most of the Jews were so insular that many could hardly speak Polish! Certainly few could read the language. Yiddish in their everyday life, Hebrew in the schools and cheiders and schuls was the accepted means of communication. Luzer had no iniquitous pursuits. He drank rarely, only ever gambled on local events that occurred mainly on an annual basis, and harboured no desires for other women.

Occasionally, when not exhausted by the labours of the day, he would join friends in a game of cards, his only hobby outside the pursuit of happiness with his wife and new-born son. Once a week, usually on a Sunday evening, Estera-Laja would wrap the baby up warm and accompany her husband to the hall at the back of the schul where they would meet with friends and dance a little to the violin strings of Yankel, the local solid-fuel deliverer. Their biggest problem was, of course, money. The incidental work that Zeider Lisner gave them was too infrequent to earn a regular and liveable wage in the winter, and procuring sufficient contracts for decorating during the short summer months was a constant headache. Heating too was of major concern to the industrious Luzer. The small house, with its one living room and tiny workmanlike kitchen downstairs and two bedrooms on the first floor, was like an ice box, unless the cooker, fuelled by solid coke, was kept aflame for the whole day. Rising in the mornings to windows that were caked in ice and rooms that you could freeze a chicken in was the most unpleasant part of their existence. In 1928, following three years of miscarriages, Estera-Laja gave birth to her second child, a girl, Basza-Hendle. Being from a most religious family, Zeider Duvid Lisner blessed the girl into the world and took her loveliness into his heart. He rejoiced at each offspring, for there were four brothers and one sister to Luzer, each of whom had several children. Zeider Duvid would make each daughter-in-law feel beautiful and fulfilled each time they gave him another grandchild. After another miscarriage, Estera-Laja and Luzer added to their family with one son and two daughters, the last born in 1934. Charmel Herch became the brother that Fiszel wanted, six years after his own birth, and Toba-Chaja and Sura-Faiga the further sisters to whom Fiszel became surrogate father and sometimes mother, for Estera-Laja was now a very sick woman.

Having learned to read and write, a unique achievement, Fiszel at ten years of age was approaching that time when boys left their schools and set about bringing some much needed money into the household. His days were filled with helping in his grandfather's butcher shop or mixing the paint and paste for his father, when the latter had been able to persuade someone that their home needed refurbishment. With a family of five children and an ailing wife, Luzer was totally embroiled in the needs of his family. He depended on his eldest boy, and while Fiszel helped all he could, bearing in mind that he too had obligations to his forthcoming barmitzvah, Luzer tended the children and his wife, as well as working all the hours that could be humanly managed. Life became tougher as Estera-Laja sought her bed, unable to assist in the daily requirements of her children and in the needs of her caring husband. With a short Mufta Haftorah, the boy Fiszel sang his barmitzvah prayers to the congregation in a fine alto voice and to the exceptional pride of his father. He was deprived of the attention of his mother who was too sick to attend the schul and hear her eldest chant his way to manhood. Many friends came back to the small house and huddled together in freezing conditions to celebrate the confirmation. Each brought a present, and many food, to adorn the barmitzvah table. Luzer was thankful that he had such caring friends for he would not have been able to afford a worthy spread. Among the presents were envelopes which contained small amounts of cash. They were opened later and used for the needs of the family. It was 1937.

They say that ignorance is bliss. The poverty that prevented the Lisners from following the dramatic events in Poland and in many other countries in Europe rendered them ignorant of the uproar against their race that was increasing daily in neighbouring Germany. In their own country, political battles with the Third Reich and with neighbouring Russia threatened their well-being, but only rumour distracted them from the daily needs for survival. Some of the extremities of Nazi propaganda were relayed to them in the monthly magazine, but these were sparse, incorrectly reported and ill-informed. And in any case, as Fiszel so sublimely put it, 'Who could believe such things?'

During the first 16 years of Fiszel's life he was unaware of the events that would determine his fate.

Hitler's release from prison and the publication of his book, *Mein Kampf*, was widely reported, for although the Nazi party had less power and support, there was little doubt that its leader would once again try to rally the German people to his way of thinking. Dissatisfaction with the Weimar Republic continued on a grand scale, even though the economy was steadily improving by way of financial assistance from the American government. A strange, complicated method of reparation payments by the German government to the French, English and Italians had evolved. Because the Americans did not agree with the terms of the armistice of 1919, the Versailles Treaty, they contracted enormous trade agreements with the Germans backed up by preferential loans that would enable the Weimar to make payments on time. When the Allies received such payments, they in turn were able to meet the interest and capital repayments that they owed America for war loans Incredibly, the Americans were therefore receiving repayments with their own money! The people of Germany were not impressed, even though prosperity similar to that enjoyed before the commencement of the First World War was the result. It was the other terms of the Versailles Treaty that left them without hope and with their Aryan pride severely dented. The limitations to armed forces. The occupation by the Allied forces of important areas of their country, particularly in the border region of the Rhineland. Then there were new borders. The corridor through Danzig was out of bounds. Czechoslovakian territory ranged deep into Germany in the south east and Austria was an independent nation. All of those areas were inhabited by Germanic peoples. It was little wonder that the Germans were hostile to the treaty.

Factions of extremists to the right and left of the centre-right power in Government continually offered their disapproval. The times were perfect for a saviour. Chancellor after chancellor stood down, unable to implement their policies in the Reichstag, for even then, before the rise of the tyrant, there were sympathisers actually sitting in the House. The Catholic centre harboured many who felt that a nationalist policy should be adopted against the smug English and intransigent French. Only the Italians, among the former Allies, shared Germany's discontent. They felt that payment for their support in the war had not been sufficiently rewarded, and as their press played upon the unequal terms of the treaty, so they too suffered from frequently-changing administrations and popular unrest. In the east the revolution of the Russian people had resulted in the formation of a Communist hard-line government which met in 1920 in order to bind nearby nations to their Bolshevik way of indoctrination. The Second Congress of the Third Republic met in Moscow and decreed the future for their neighbours. Poland, amongst many others, not inclined to adopt an authoritarian attitude of such magnitude as preached by Marx and Lenin. Only the Jewish foreign minister of the Soviets, Litvinov, pleaded for a more restrained approach to Communist policy and an awareness, when confronting the right wing factions, of other countries.

He meant Germany!

That the Second World War was a delayed product of the terms of the Versailles Treaty, or because Germany never accepted the responsibility of blame, or even that they actually lost the war, is a matter for historians. What was undoubtedly true was the charisma of one man in all the upheaval and disagreement. As the years between the wars passed, so he gathered supporters like a rolling stone.

Every adverse event was exploited to the full by Hitler until he gathered sufficient backing to warrant election to Weimar. Hindenberg, the President, refuted his acclaim. He failed to recognise opportunism. The real opportunity came from an event several thousand miles away during October 1929. The month of the Wall Street crash. Within a year the Americans had abolished their loans policy. Germany missed a payment to France. The French sent an army into the Rhineland to occupy the steel factories and coal mines to gain reparation by seconding those goods. The mark fell. The mark fell again. Inflation raged. Unemployment went from 2,800,000 in 1928 to 6,000,000 in 1930. Chancellors came and went. The navy revolted. The army withdrew support. Local political parties declared unilateral independence from Berlin. It mattered not whether they were on the right or the left. The seven years of improvement in the economy prior to 1929 went out of the window. The Nazi party increased its representation in the Reichstag to a third of the total members. It expounded its Nationalist policies with vast expenditure on propaganda. The people actually believed that the Jewish Communists were responsible for all their woes. Naturally, they agreed with the withholding of all future reparation payments and the build-up of illegal military might. German might. Hitler decreed that when he was in power all the men would be in employment in order to restore the pride in the German family.

Whether he meant this and other declarations is not known, except to say that under his rule the economy improved a thousand fold, and gross unemployment disappeared. It certainly is known that his missives were of popular appeal to many levels of society. Industrialists, bankers and professional people were now numbered among his supporters. The memory of how his party had started, as the Munich Workers Union, had been conveniently forgotten. Some will say that the economy was already improving when, in 1933, Hitler took control and declared himself chancellor. Hindenberg was dying and Hitler seized this opportunity to claim extraordinary rights not afforded his predecessors. Elections followed. The results were unimportant as his stormtroopers prevented the elected Democrats from taking their seats anyway!

Hitler, in an effort to appease fearful industrialists, then killed many of his former supporters in the Night of the Long Knives. They were not charged with disloyalty, but he saw their power-hungry presence as a threat, for the party was not one of absolute unity. Not, that is, until his submissive and conditioned faithfuls were the only ones remaining.

Hitler's incredible rise to power caused anxiety in the west, and indeed many of the neighbouring countries were wary of the new leader. His was not the usual political party.

Emblems, slogans, uniforms and Swastikas screamed at visitors and dignitaries alike.

It is little wonder that the cultured Chamberlain, the Prime Minister of England, regarded his adversary with fear and unfounded respect. The use of violence was not the normal instrument of a democratic government. Establishment of power and popularity was normally achieved by discussion and implementation of popular policies. Hitler's method was to hold large open-air meetings in city squares, where he would whip up support in a frenzy of rhetoric, and then have his stormtroopers beat up and kill dissenters and opponents. The message was simple and appealing. 'The Allies, with the aid of wealthy Jews and Jewish Communists in Germany have conspired to keep Germany weak by way of the Versailles Treaty. Rally now behind the leader and destroy all the internal enemies, and then seek the return of those lands that truly belong to

Germany'.

While he was convincing his people of this, he also reorganised production in hundreds of engineering and chemical factories to commence making previously banned, illegal weapons. Surreptitiously and incredibly, he began to build up his armed forces in direct contravention to his predecessor's undertakings. France panicked. Britain looked toward the Empire for economic support, turning its back on the activities of the dictator. The fact that *Mein Kampf* and openly-pronounced policies centred around the increasing of agriculturally productive land, belonging now to the Poles and the Czechs, made little impression on the British. Even the declaration that they were involved with an international conspiracy of Jews and Communists to overrun Germany in the not too distant future made little impression on the isolationist policies expressed by the British Parliament.

'If it isn't at the doors of Westminster then is of little concern to us!' Ah, how Parliament will always regret that attitude.

Under the Fascist regime Germany began to prosper, along with the rest of Europe that had suffered from the effects of the American depression. It was the United States itself that was taking the longest time to feel the warm winds of recovery.

During my many discussions with Fiszel, I continually pressed him for details of his awareness of what was happening to Poland and the rest of Europe. How he felt about the news that surely filtered through. I was disappointed that his comments were vague and uninformative, but I respected the fact that when Hitler assumed power, Fiszel was just nine years old. It was likely that the adult but insular Jews of the region were far more aware of what was happening all around them.

Nevertheless, I am forced to wonder whether they knew that eight months after Hitler's accession, in October 1933, Germany withdrew from the League of Nations Disarmament Conference and threatened the country's resignation from the League.

Three months after that, in January 1934, Fiszel's homeland, Poland, actually signed a ten-year non-aggression pact with the Third Reich.

Seven months thereafter, in July, there was an attempted Nazi coup in Austria, resulting in the murder of Chancellor Dollfuss.

One month later Hindenberg died and left the mantle of supremacy to the tyrant, who then declared himself Fuhrer.

He followed this act with a command to all military personnel that they must swear allegiance and loyalty to their new 'Emperor', in the first instance, and to the Fatherland thereafter.

While I question the awareness of the Jewish people resident in Szeracz, I am also inclined to question the sanity of the Fuhrer at this time. Had megalomania set in? Was he even mentally fit to run the country? Subsequent events may tell the reader that there is much credence to my doubt.

The States of Europe continued to blunder their way through to their ultimate goals, mindless of the threat, mindless of the military build-up and mindless of the massive increase in arms production. Meeting after meeting took place, often with one or more of the protagonists walking out prior to any conclusion.

For reasons best known to themselves, Russia decided to replace Germany in the League of Nations. That took place in September 1934. Quite independently, but possibly with Nazi support, a Croatian Fascist then decided to murder the French Foreign Minister, Barthou, and also the King of Yugoslavia, Alexander, during a meeting at Marseilles.

What was the motive of the Saar people, located in the west of Germany, south-east of Belgium, who were enjoying a form of independence, to vote overwhelmingly to incorporate themselves into mainland Germany? Where were the French, the British, the Italians? Everything that had been agreed in the Versailles Treaty was falling down around them. Was the time not right for reprisal, before any further dangerous decisions could be made by the Nazis? The opportunity was missed, and lost forever, when Goebbels publicly announced the Fatherland's intention to establish a military force by way of conscription which would arm Germany with a further 36 divisions. Did the Allies not know that at least half of these had already been established by the time Goebbels made this most significant public announcement in March 1935?

The Allies did react! They met in Stresa, condemned the announcement and confirmed their interest in the continuing independence of Austria, then went home.

Hitler laughed and was allowed to carry on in his own less than sweet way. A pact between France and Russia followed, one month later, in May 1935, and in June Britain saw fit to sign a naval agreement whose terms provided for a limited increase in the Fatherland's navy, to 35 per cent of the British surface fleet, and 45 per cent of her submarine fleet. Hitler was already known to have scant regard for agreements, and it remains as totally unbelievable that the British Government could honestly have expected the Fuhrer to honour this latest pact. It surely must be concluded that obdurate disregard, rather than naivety, was the motivation behind such innocence. How did they react when Italy, now being governed by Mussolini, invaded Abyssinia only three months later? Newsreels had shown the two Fascist leaders as close allies, sharing a common pursuit, with a common authoritarian doctrine.

When France and England decided to agree to a partition of

Abyssinia-after all, Italy was their former ally-the news of the decision leaked out and Foreign Secretary Hoare was forced to resign. Perhaps, in order to deflect blame from his own critics (was it he who leaked the news?), French Prime Minister Laval immediately turned his attention to the Russians and ratified a pact with them.

It seems that practically every country in Europe was running around signing meaningless pacts in one of the most confusing periods of political history.

We are now into February 1936, and one month later, in an act of retaliation for the French Government's deviousness, the Germans re-militarised the Rhineland and for the first time since 1918, they were in direct confrontation with the French. Missing from all this historical litany of events were the Portuguese, the Greeks and the Spanish. If Italy and Germany could have Fascist domination, so could they. Franco, yet another right wing extremist, challenged the Royal Household's authority, and the Spanish Civil War commenced in July 1936. Spurred on by the line of least resistance being offered by his former enemies, Hitler instructed Goering to 'Prepare Germany for a state of war within four years'. Three months after that, in November 1936, Germany made friends with the Japanese who were causing political embarrassment to the Americans in Manchuria and China. Between that event and the subsequent invasion by the Japanese, in July 1937, Neville Chamberlain succeeded Baldwin as British Prime Minister. As if there wasn't sufficient turmoil amongst the nations, Il Duce took Italy out of the League of Nations (Hitler's instigation?), and subsequently persuaded the new British Prime Minister to recognise his authority over Abyssinia. Poor old Anthony Eden, the British Foreign Secretary. He was diametrically opposed to such acquiescence and duly resigned. Notwithstanding a number of further meetings and pacts, all of which subsequently proved to be of little import, September 1938 arrived with frantic meetings between Hitler and Chamberlain at Berchtesgaden and Bad Godesberg, after which a further meeting was arranged, this time to include the French and the Italians. The pressure of Hitler's extraordinary charisma and growing influence, must have affected their judgement. They agreed that the Fuhrer could indeed have the Sudeten area of Czechoslovakia, and to appoint a commission to examine all of Hitler's remaining complaints about the Germanic peoples who lived under alien rulers. Not happy with this, the Slovaks announced their independence from the Czechs, and Hitler invaded their country. March 1939. Then the ambitious Fuhrer decided to turn his attention to the east, and the port of Memel in Lithuania fell into his hands. A seaway on the Baltic! It then became evident that Hitler must have designs on Poland in order to create a corridor through Danzig.

He needed just one further treaty to have everything in place. Russia! A plan to dissect Poland down the middle from north to south was devised, and a non-aggression pact between the two countries was signed. All the Polish wealth east of Warsaw would soon become an extension to Russia, while the western regions would provide the Third Reich with everything that Hitler desired: the aforementioned corridor to the Baltic, a work force of Jewish slaves, coal mines, and invaluable agricultural land. Everything was set for the war of all wars, and for the elimination of 6,000,000 Jews in what we now call the Holocaust. For five long years evil would reign over good, Satan over the Lord, and many of the peoples of the world would suffer as never before.

In Ulicia-Szerazka, Number 28, according to Fiszel, life continued at an even pace. They were only marginally aware of the Polish armies who gathered to resist, as the cavalry paraded along the 3,000 miles of border surrounding their country, confident that their superior numbers of 45 divisions would be all that was needed to drive the enemy from their lands.

On 1 September, 1939, in defiance of the warnings of Neville Chamberlain, 30 divisions of the Third Reich moved into Poland. ThePoles found their lofty steeds no match for the modern weapons of their enemy.

A horse against a tank was to offer little resistance.

Four days after this event, the first sound of bombs and shelling echoed in the ears of the frightened people, Catholics and Jews alike, who, in near equal numbers, inhabited the Town of Zdunska-Wola.

CHAPTER 3

THE EARLY DESPERATE YEARS 1939-1940

While Fiszel can find no forgiveness in his heart for what the Nazis did to him, his family and his country, he accepts the reasoning behind the sporadic persecution of Jews within Poland prior to the German invasion. When Hitler signed his ten-year non-aggression pact with Poland in January 1934, it must be accepted that the sympathisers of the nationalist policies of their neighbours would attract a number of members of the community. Fiszel himself was never a subject of violence because of his race, and indeed, until the arrival of the Wehrmacht in his town, had a number of Catholic associates. Friends would be the incorrect label for them because they too enjoyed their own kind. Generally, save for a few extremists in both communities, the two peoples of Poland survived with passive acceptance of each other. They traded together and with each other. They worked in each other's establishments and occasionally shared communal pastimes.

As the years after the agreement passed, so the right wing factions hardened. The growth of the Third Reich and the widely advertised policies of its Fuhrer were bound to attract sympathizers in other countries. Poland was no exception.

Throughout these years it became increasingly less safe for unaccompanied Jews to venture out of their houses at night. More frequent indiscriminate attacks took place, and the divisive line between the races grew ever wider. In the United States the Klu Klux Klan found much support. In Italy the Fascists under Mussolini warmed to their leader and cooled towards the Jews. In the less cosmopolitan areas of France, people voiced and practised varying degrees of intolerance.

In England the member of parliament Sir Oswald Moseley championed the Fascist cause with rallies and meetings that gathered to him many supporters whose beliefs had previously been shrouded under the guise of patriotism and affection for the Royal Household. The Astors, a powerful and wealthy aristocratic business and political family, opposed all forms of liberal thinking, courted Hitler, and expressed hatred for the ebullient Churchill. Rumania, Lithuania and the Croatian element of Jugoslavia also savoured the winds of acceptance to anti-semitism generated from the central force that was the Government of Germany. That is, until the Germans signed the treaty with Russia on 23 August 1939, and threw the Poles into a state of confusion. They were previously tolerant of the suppression that was going on. It suited the pact. They had an agreement. It is interesting to note that there were many thousands of Jews serving in their armed forces at the outbreak of war. It may then be seen that the Polish attitude no longer mattered. The enemy was a territory seeker and the anti-semitism was inconsequential to the desire of the Fuhrer. Poland was to be dissected between the Russians and the Germans, and they were forced to organise defences of their borders around the whole perimeter of the country. They turned to England and France and for once the British jumped off the fence and publicly declared their support, should Germany invade. Words came easily!

Fiszel stood with his family and the family of Yankel the coal man, watching the first squadrons of bombers pass overhead, on their way to the capital, Warsaw, on that fateful day. Josef, Yankel's eldest son and Fiszel's closest friend, shook with fear as he clutched the arm of his friend, when the first bombs were dropped on Zdunska-Wola. One of these made a direct hit on the large house on the far corner of their street, which was where the landlord of the many terraced and tenement houses and flats, lived. He was in the house and was instantly killed. After the final bomber had passed over, the hundreds of Jews who lined the streets returned to their homes and to the synagogue to await the news that would be spread among the community by the elders. It was the first occasion that Fiszel can remember taking an active interest in the events that preceded the raid. Comments, discussion, argument and rumour raged among his peers until Tuesday 5 September, following many more air strikes on Warsaw, Lodz and Zdunska-Wola. All rumour ceased when his father awoke him to join him in the main street, across several alleyways and back yards, to watch the arrival of the Wehrmacht. Armoured cars, with machine guns pointing forward, small tanks with helmeted commanders leaning out of the turret, and trucks full of young soldiers passed in convoy on their way to the market square in the town centre. Fear struck in their hearts. The adults and senior members of the community had become fully aware of the atrocities that were taking place in neighbouring Germany. Many relatives had found their way from their homes in Germany to Polish border towns in the two years and recent months before the invasion. Fiszel was commanded to pack everything that he could lay his hands on onto the horse and cart that his family owned and to make ready to walk to his uncle and aunty who lived with their two daughters in Lodz.

I asked him why his father chose to go further inland toward the east. Was it that he thought that they would escape from the invaders if he headed away from Germany?

As far as Fiszel could remember, his father explained that it would be good for the family to be together. That seemed to be his only reason. He could not know that there was no escape. No collective remission from the horrors that were about to unfold. For two days the horse plodded along the road carrying their goods in the cart while the children walked alongside. Many of their neighbours had chosen to do the same. They were like a nomadic caravan in the desert, seeking freedom in a place that would soon be as constrictive as the place they had deserted. They reached Lodz on Thursday the seventh. On Friday the eighth the Wehrmacht and the S.S. arrived there, just as they had done in Zdunska-Wola. The Lisners stayed for three days only and then returned to their home town. When they arrived they were informed by public notices pinned to trees and walls everywhere, and by those that had not tried to seek refuge elsewhere, that they had to go to the town hall and register their family as Jews.

"What is that on your coat?" Fiszel enquired of his friend Josef.

He had seen the yellow arm band, sewn onto the boy's coat sleeve, that had been issued to all Jews.

When he arrived at the town hall there were long lines of Jews from all parts of the town, waiting to register with the German clerks who sat at desks in the foyer of the auditorium. Many of the Jews who were at the end of the queues were lying on the ground with their faces turned to the earth. Fiszel and his father joined the queues, immediately being directed to lay on the ground until they crawled nearer to the steps of the town hall, when they would be allowed to rise. His mother was too sick to attend. His sisters too frail and too young. Luzer hoped that the Germans would not insist that he bring the stricken woman to the square. After four hours of slowly crawling nearer the hall in the harsh autumn conditions, Luzer's turn to register finally came. He was told to stand to one side pending further questioning. The instruction was clear. All Jews must register and show themselves personally. Fiszel waited for his father outside the square, lonely and frightened and aware that the vicious interrogators were powerful enough to imprison his father without reference to the boy and without even telling him what they had done. In the dark evening he shivered and waited. His mind dwelt on the news that Josef had given him when he arrived back from Lodz.

"All the owners of the textile factories and the big wholesalers on the corner have been ejected from their offices and their homes and thrown in prison."

"I know, Josef. I have already seen my Zeider and he has told me that the Germans closed his kosher butcher shop as soon as they arrived."

Had Luzer, too, been cast away, never to be seen again? Fiszel's mind raced over the responsibilities that would face him as the eldest member of his family.

He had been out in the cold, suffering from the winds and the snow, for seven and one half hours, when Luzer reappeared. His father had been questioned unmercifully, but eventually they decided to allow him to leave, only because he told them that by trade he was a building worker, but in the winter months he purchased live animals for slaughter which were used in part by his grandfather, but many cuts of meat went to the non-kosher butcher, Tadek, a friendly Pole. Luzer explained that Jews did not eat the rump of animals. This infuriated his inquisitors, because, by implication, the Gentiles ate the arse end of the animals while the Jews retained the prime meat for themselves. This intrigued the senior officer who was dressed in the macabre uniform of the S.S.. He certainly would have preferred to beat the insolent Jew who stood before him, but the man would be useful in obtaining the supplies that they would need, and so Luzer was spared.

Father and son hugged each other and cried their relief onto each other's shoulders, oblivious of the falling temperature and the swirling winds.

The next day, after all the Jews had been told not to go to their work stations anymore, after all Jewish-owned shops had been closed down, and after many more independent traders had been arrested, Luzer was awarded a licence to continue to leave Zdunska-Wola so he could visit the surrounding villages to purchase cattle for the troops and German Poles only. No meat was to be supplied to the Jews. It was made very clear that if he was caught selling meat to anyone other than those nominated he would be shot immediately. But Luzer was an obstinate man. A man who had defied convention when he elected to earn his living by way of self-employment. He called on local Polish (as distinct from German Polish), allotment owners, farmers and market gardeners. Each in turn was happy to sell him what he desired. Their sales were being increased ten-fold, and the prospect of sudden wealth, improved by additional sales and black-market prices, was a boon to their previously meagre existence.

It was an ill wind!

As the horse slowly plodded its way back toward the place where Luzer would unload to the German guards, many of his friends would be at the end of their small yards waiting with hidden Zlotis to buy potatoes and turnips and beetroot from him as he passed by. Hundreds of Jews, denied income, work and food, began dealing from his mobile cart. The effect was to keep them from starving, but also to make Luzer wealthier than he had ever been. His own outside pantry, cellar and hidden cupboards became crammed with garden-fresh vegetables, prime meat and money. Fiszel, when he was unable to persuade the guards that he was needed to accompany his father on these forays into the surrounding countryside, was given the task of street cleaning. Josef, his friend, had particular responsibility for the stables, the manure and the boots of the soldiers who still used equine transport. He became the subject of their ridicule, for he was not a brave boy, or a strong-minded one, and his eager, naive simplicity was apparent to all who spoke to him. Many times during their friendship, Fiszel had needed to use his own strength and prowess to bail the boy out of some form of trouble. Even at the Jewish school, Josef was regarded as an easy touch, a subject of banter and ridicule. He countered this with his own sense of humour, which was always evident in his conversation. Fiszel thought that he would have made a very good Jewish comic, for he saw humour in all things. Later, this sense of the ridiculous was to cost him his life. As the level of oppression grew, as many more of the Jews were taken away for questioning, mostly never to be seen again, so life became increasingly more difficult. By November all public facilities and places of interest were banned to the Jews. They were not allowed to worship in their temples. All the Jewish schools were closed down. The doctors and nurses and dentists among them were in the main prevented from practising their professions, and medical supplies dwindled so that people like Estera-Laja, who needed constant attention, became more ill, and many died from neglect and the absence of drugs and treatment.

It was also during that November that the Jews of Zdunska-Wola were ordered to gather in the town square, over a period of three days. The square effectively held, maybe, 10,000 people. There were 26,000 in the town. At the first gatherings they were told to leave their homes and belongings that they were unable to carry or cart, and to move into a part of the town that was known to be the poorest of all the residential areas. The Zdunska-Wola ghetto was to be set up, with all Jews ordered to live in one district. A use for the now defunct school rooms had been found. In three journeys, the Lisner family managed to move all of their clothing and personal effects and the two beds that they would need. Under each mattress were piles of vegetables, meat and money. Fortunately, none of the guards who hurried them along bothered to peer under the beds, upon one of which lay the now seriously ill Estera-Laja. And so they were able to smuggle much food into the small classroom which they and two further families were forced to inhabit. The room had previously been a school room for about ten students. There were now 24 people living in it!

It was in that same month that Fiszel and his sisters and one brother lay on the end of their mother's death bed, their father, a neighbour and a nurse in attendance to hear the 36year-old woman's last words. "Luzer, the children watch my face. Turn their heads away from me, so that they do not see my despair."

These were her last words. An onlooker might have been forgiven if he had concluded that the dying woman was nearer to 56 years of age. Only when the peace of death entered her soul did the deep lines of pain and anguish leave her face.

She was buried in the Jewish cemetery, not yet demolished and destroyed, with many of their friends and neighbours in attendance and the Rabbi nervously saying the last rites, ever watchful for a gang of hooligans, or German soldiers, who might approach and desecrate the proceedings. Because Luzer and Fiszel were needed each day to carry out their tasks, they were not allowed to sit 'shiver', the one week of mourning, but after hours, many more than the ten men that are required for a 'Minion' (a seven-night gathering of ten men to mourn the departed), gathered at their home to say their mournful prayers.

"Vayisgadow, Vayishtabuch", they chanted in muted voices for the passing of the once beautiful girl who had given birth to five children and who had been at her husband's side, ever aware of her family's needs and her obligations, and who had passed on during what should have been the prime period of her life, with only unselfish thoughts of her children and her loving husband.

It was not then known that her passing was what the Jews call a 'Mitzvah', a blessing in disguise.

It was in January 1940 that Luzer stopped at a house almost at the end of the alleyway that led to the market square, to off-load some potatoes for a few extra Zlotis. A lone Wehrmacht soldier peered into the alleyway to observe his illegal black marketeering. According to Fiszel, who heard the story from Luzer sometime later, the soldier was a very young man and did not seem inclined to use his bayonet, bullets or the butt of his rifle. Instead he held Luzer's arm as he guided him into the square, where he asked one of his colleagues to take the horse and cart and its contents to the warehouse, while he took Luzer inside to the town Commandant.

It was a day when Fiszel was working on the drains, clearing the filters under ground from the excrement and rubbish that blocked them. When he arrived home one of the other residents told him what had happened.

Fiszel cooked the supper for his younger sisters and brother, all the time perspiring and worrying about the fate of his father. At ten o'clock that same night, Luzer returned battered and bruised from repeated beatings. He had lost his licence and the horse and cart. Both he and Fiszel would be required to work in future on the construction of the new barracks at the edge of the town. At least Luzer was alive!

The next evening, following his first day on the building site, where he was hod-carrying for most of the day, Fiszel left his room to take some food hidden in his boots to his Zeider Duvid. When he arrived at his grandparents' cellar residence it was deserted and he was told that his Zeider and his Booba had been taken away during the night along with many other old and infirm residents in that part of the ghetto.

To this day Fiszel has no idea what happened to them. They were never to be seen again. We can guess.

Somehow, by devious means, Luzer managed to keep his family fed and watered, and continued to sell and buy small quantities of additional supplies. Fiszel remembers his father coming home one day with a bag of rice. Another time he came back from his day's labours with a bag of flour. The baker in the ghetto paid handsomely for the opportunity to make more bread in one day than he had ever previously managed. Fiszel, too, managed to befriend one of the kitchen porters, a German Pole, who worked in the canteen that serviced the Jewish workers on the building site with one bowl of soup and a slice of black bread each day. With a few Zlotis here and there, Fiszel purchased some extra crumbs to add to the meagre allowances that had been allowed to his family by way of rationing. By the end of March the barracks had been completed.

Several workers were not allowed to leave the site as usual that last night. Luzer was one that would be retained. Fiszel asked whether he could be the substitute for his father as the older man was needed at the ghetto to attend the children.

"You can come too", the S.S. guard informed him.

There were seven men in a line. An equal number of Wehrmacht and S.S. guards faced them. Their leader was smiling.

"You", pointing to Luzer. "Come forward." Luzer stepped one pace. "Another step."

Luzer moved further forward cautiously, fear on his face.

"You asked whether there would be some pay for your work, Jude?"

Luzer nodded.

"Here is your pay."

The S.S. officer turned, laughed, and beckoned to two Wehrmacht and one S.S. soldier. Fiszel stood, screaming inside of his stomach, closing his eyes in terror and disbelief, horror and shock, as the three brutes beat his father with the butts of their rifles and their Luger pistols, until Luzer fell to the ground, semi-conscious, bloody and battered. With some final kicks into his head and side and stomach, the three men retreated.

"Take your father with you Jude, before you get the same!"

Somehow, with sheer strength of character, determination and love for his father, Fiszel managed to drag and carry the inert form the three kilometres to the town, through the square back to the ghetto. In normal circumstances, a beating like that would have needed several weeks of recuperation. It was only three days later that Luzer was ordered to attend another site where construction was taking place and his services and that of his son would be required.

In March of that same year, the first wave (transport) of workers needed to help with the construction of the proposed autobahn between Berlin and Warsaw were loaded into trucks and taken away from the town. They were mostly men and boys between the ages of 12 and 40. In May a second transport was required for the same work. Luzer was ordered to gather with others at the office hut on the edge of the ghetto with some belongings. Fiszel argued and pleaded that he should be the one to go, as his sisters needed their father more than he. They surely would perish without his father's secret dealings and ability to find food and supplies. At eight o'clock that morning Fiszel left home with Luzer's reluctant acquiescence and attended the chosen point. The German-Polish civilian who was taking down the names of the transportees made no mention of the fact that Fiszel had replaced Luzer.

The clerk's indifference and Fiszel's unselfishness was, in retrospect, to be of momentous importance.

Josef was among the transportees, although he was shepherded into a truck other than the one which carried Fiszel to the site. For two days they rode in the back of the crowded vehicle, never once being allowed to stop for food or water, or to relieve themselves. The trucks did stop, there were five of them, several times, but they were advised that if any of them left the vehicles, for any reason whatsoever, they would be shot.

In the mid-afternoon on the second day they arrived at a nameless site that Fiszel later learned was inside Poland just east of Wloclawek, east of the river Vistula.

They dismounted, stiff and hungry, and queued to register with one of the guards. Josef waved to Fiszel, and hoped that they would be billeted together. It was not to be.

Fiszel was ordered into one of the low-roofed, single-storey, wooden-constructed, unheated billets that formed a semi-circle around the perimeter of the site, along with a neighbour from Zdunska-Wola who he knew well, Chaim Ber Urbach. He was to be the billet supervisor. Later they were to be told what that meant in terms of responsibility. Josef waved again from across the yard as he followed his own small party to their designated billet.

The sparsely furnished room had four double bunks in it, two buckets, a wooden table and one chair. There was no sink, or toilet, or lockers to hang clothes on, or drawers to house underwear and personal possessions. Fiszel followed the others by leaving his clothing in his case and slumping down on the hard horse hair mattress. It was covered with just one blanket. Just a few minutes later, a guard entered and ordered them to line up in the open area in front of the guards' building for roll call. To make four lines of 50 and not to speak. Josef looked for Fiszel and somehow managed to weave his way to the position immediately to the left of his friend. They lined up in the waning evening light and waited. For one hour they stood in silence. Then, a row of about 20 soldiers, fronted by four S.S. officers, formed a line in front of them. Josef could not resist a sideways comment. Fiszel cannot remember exactly what the boy said, but it was one of his many jokes.

It was to cost him his life.

"What did you say?" the senior officer enquired.

Josef said nothing. Fiszel glanced down at the ground.

"Step forward", the officer commanded.

Josef meekly took a small step forward.

The officer then broke into a stream of foul language, much of which the frightened Jews failed to understand. Josef was shaking, unable to move, transfixed to the spot where he was standing, in front of and close to the line of soldiers.

"You Jude next to him. Come forward."

Fiszel stepped forward.

"Hit him!" the officer commanded.

Fiszel pushed Josef on the shoulder.

"Again! Harder!", the S.S. officer commanded.

Fiszel shoved Josef playfully.

"Not like that, Jude fool. Like this!" he screamed. At that point he turned and snatched a rifle out of the hands of one of the soldiers. In similar fashion to a baseball player attempting to knock the ball out of the ground, he swung the rifle towards Josef's head. At the final moment, he twisted the gun so that the flat surface of the butt pointed skywards and the sharp half-inch thick side of the butt slammed into Josef's head. The crack that resulted caused many of the onlookers to physically vomit, as did the sight of Josef's blood, flesh, brains and particles of bone spattered over the rifle and on Fiszel's coat. Josef slumped to the ground after the force of the blow had knocked him sideways into Fiszel.

Fiszel's clothes were covered with his friend's remains, for he was dead before he had even bumped into him.

Laughing, the officer plunged the rifle into Fiszel's hand, challengingly, and ordered him to wipe the butt on his friend's clothing. For just one moment, one moment in time, the world stood still for Fiszel Lisner. The temptation to turn the rifle onto the officer was overwhelming, but he didn't know how to release the safety catch or even how to fire the gun.

He did as he was bade, the tears flowing from his eyes, his heart torn out, his soul destroyed.

It was then that I asked Fiszel, as gently as I could, "Do you remember your feelings at that time?"

He looked at me, stubbed out the cigarette, and answered very slowly.

"Do you think that I could ever forget such a thing?"

Falteringly, he recalled that moment.

Inadequately, I will try to explain it to you.

As Fiszel bent to clear the bloodstains and flesh from the butt of the rifle, his legs turned to jelly and his resolve diminished. For one moment, and perhaps for the first of many times to come, he wished that he too was dead. Then, fear of such proportion entered his soul that his face turned ashen white and his head began to swim. He could feel himself rolling forward. He knew in his heart that if he collapsed he would surely die, if not from anguish and despair, then from the wrath of his German tormentors. Was it the face of Estera-Laja? Was it his brother or his sisters, or perhaps Luzer, who called him to return his mind to the clarity that was needed in order to save his life? He stretched out a hand and prevented himself from falling all the way forward, making it appear that it was no more than a support needed for balance. Throughout the ensuing 15 minutes, while the commandant spoke threateningly of retribution for attempted escape, for theft, even of a slice of bread, for insolence and disobedience, he resisted the vomit and bile that was trying to force its way out of his nauseous belly. Forcibly and furiously he controlled these natural and understandable urges, growing in courage and sensing a return to his resolve. It was then that he knew that he would never see his family again. The thought entered his mind like a steam train at full speed. It was as if a message had been passed to him.

'Stay alive. You must fight for your survival.'

Fiszel Lisner was 16 going on 60!

Josef, who was the same age, would never see another day.

Perhaps, bearing in mind what we now know, he was the lucky one.

At this point in relating his story, Fiszel stopped and lit one of his frequent Benson and Hedges. I turned off the cassette recorder and joined him. Mrs Miller, Fiszel's long standing friend, business partner and housekeeper, who was listening in, rose from the table at which we were sitting, awkwardly, desperately trying to avoid the embarrassment of tears, and left the room in silence. Fiszel and I remained sitting at the table, gazing out of the window, but seeing nothing, playing with the ash in the tray and saying nothing. Mary returned with two coffees and Fiszel and I continued to smoke and drink in absolute silence. I could go no further. I was too distraught.

It must have been all of 20minutes before I felt sufficiently in control of my emotions to gather up my pen and to write.

For Fiszel Lisner, it was 52 years on. It was the first time that he had ever told anyone this story. Many had asked. Only now, in the late evening of his life, did he feel ready to speak.

For me, I had never heard such a tale. Oh yes, I have read and read until I could not keep my eyes open, of the atrocities of the Second World War, but never have I been told of an inhuman act by a man who lived it, who saw it with his own eyes, who was actually there, a part of it, as it took place.

Never have I felt the pain so acutely. The writing of this biography was proving to be far more difficult than I at first realised. I knew that there would be pain. Foolishly, I thought that the pain would be that of the subject's, not that of the biographer.

I felt humbled. And in a strange way, honoured.

I wondered whether Fiszel was feeling relief, or was the memory now just a distant nightmare that had plundered all the emotion from him. I dare not ask. I stared at him in wonderment.

I sat there thinking of the many books to which I had been referring for the purposes of research; *World War II*, by Roland Heiferman. *How War Came,* by Donald Cameron Watt. *The Origins of the Second World War,* by Ruth Henig. *The Final Journey* and *The Holocaust,* both by Martin Gilbert. The controversial litany of historical events, with almost sympathetic apologies to Hitler, called *The Origins of the Second World War,* by Britain's A. J. P. Taylor. And many, many others.

For me, I am afraid none of them made me feel really sad, depressed, anguished, crestfallen, for they are chronologies of events. Records and statements.

I do not wish to criticize my fellow authors. Far be it for me, an amateur by comparison, to offer such utterances against them, but did they ever stop and feel? Truly feel?

Will you, my readers, now place this book on the table beside you, close your eyes and feel?

Think of your own best friend and think of him being killed by another human being in a similar way to Josef. Or the way that Fiszel had to witness the event. And to clean the rifle?

Are we animals? Can any of us ever again condone the doctrines of pathologically homicidal politicians and follow them just because the objects of their wrath and inadequacies and insanities are directed against a colour, a creed, a race? Do any of us have a choice when we are brought into the world?

What divine power ordains the colour of our skin? Our political and religious inclinations? Our beliefs? Our affiliations?

It cannot be considered that the same power that determines these things, the spiritual guidance that enables us freedom of thought and action, also grants us the right to blindly hate and despise, vociferously torment, physically torture and ruthlessly murder other human beings.

Surely, we will never allow such atrocities as inflicted by the Nazis of the Third Reich to ever occur again?

CHAPTER 4

THE WORK CAMPS 1940-1943

As the black-capped, black suited S.S. officer strutted up and down the path in front of bedraggled, travel-weary prisoners, Fiszel tried desperately to bring mind, body and soul together. Josef was still lying on the ground, the red streams of the blood from his wounds just trickling now. Fiszel could make out some of the officer's words such as shot and hung, or the odd half sentence such as no escape, ten people for every attempt, etc. The man was behaving as if he was the clone of his leader, shouting, gesticulating and raising his voice to a demented scream when he needed to emphasise a particular point. How long he made them stand there listening to his diatribe Fiszel has no idea. He only became aware that the man had finished his discourse when the group of around 200 men began to form a queue at the northerly end of the camp where the kitchens were, presumably to receive some longed for sustenance. Fiszel turned and saw two of the Jews from the rear of the queue drop to their knees to remove the inert form that was once his best friend. His life long friend. The one with whom he had shared his dreams and his pranks and his hardships. Slowly the line moved forward, and eventually Fiszel arrived at the head of the long queue and was handed a small piece of bread and a container which he describes as a sort of billy can. Moving along the length of the wooden table manned by two German Polish civilians, he watched as they poured a measure of pale green liquid into the can. Slowly and disinterestedly he followed Chaim and the other six members of his billet back to seclusion. Once inside he greedily consumed the meagre piece of bread and the lukewarm soup. He remembers.

"Fiszel, you have eaten the soup and bread so quickly before I have had a chance to tell you that what you have before you now is all that you are going to get until this time tomorrow night. You should eat the soup and save the bread for lunch time tomorrow. The days will be hard and you will need some food."

Chaim then related in detail the uninvited responsibilities with which he had been burdened. All the misdemeanours of the billet would be upon his head. So no escape, no thieving, no fighting, and strict obedience to the Germans' instructions.

The inmates lay on their beds, bemused and bewildered by the suddenness in the change to their lives. All Fiszel could think of was his friend and the lingering hunger, for he was a well-built boy. Not tall, but large of bone structure.

After some considerable time, well into the night, he must have fallen asleep, because he awoke to the sound of hammering and the sound of voices calling to each other. There were two windows in the billet, one on either side of the two longer walls, so he stood on tiptoe to see what all the commotion was about. More than a 100 civilians were digging footholds for posts that would hold the mesh of wire that was being erected all around the perimeter of the camp. Inside the billet all the others had awoken and were trying to see what was happening.

Strangely, he remembers that not one word was said. With little food inside him and no sleep to speak of, he awaited the call, which he knew would be in the early hours, to once again stand in line. At six a.m. a siren sounded and almost simultaneously a Wehrmacht guard burst through the door and began prodding each man to rise and attend the line-up.

Fiszel's vision of the man, standing by the side of his bunk, teasing him that he might be the next to suffer the same fate as Josef, is as vivid as if it happened on the day he was relating this story to me. Roughly prodding and poking the inmates with his bayonet, the guard showed the small group the direction to a line of men that was already forming on the furthest side of the camp. Fiszel took his place among them, the depression of the night before still uppermost in his mind. Finally, he reached a line of about six metal troughs. Each had a cold water tap above it.

He remembers clearly the effect of the freezing water upon his hands and face. One towel was used by each complete line of men. Slowly, his stomach contracting, his muscles aching, he followed Chaim to his place in the assembly. The procedure was the same as the previous evening, the men forming four lines of approximately 50 in each. He did not welcome being in the front line. Nothing was said by either the guards or the lone S.S. officer on duty until the count was completed. Accompanied by around eight guards, heavily armed and with their bayonets fixed, the prisoners slowly followed in a long straggling line until they came to a large open area that spread, uninterrupted by tree or foliage, westward for as far as the eye could see.

The had tramped for one and a half kilometres. Each man was asked whether he was skilled, and when Fiszel told them that he had no real experience in the field of civil construction, he was handed a large shovel and told to join a group of labourers whose task it would be to dig the foundations of the planned autobahn. There were many civilians present, Germans with clip-boards, German Poles mostly to act as overseers, and pure Polish who generally were allowed to supervise small teams engaged in some of the less arduous tasks such as clearing debris, driving trucks and tractors which trailed large containers behind them. These were the only form of mechanised support on site. Chaim remained in charge of

Fiszel's group, a decision that was to benefit him sometime later when he desperately needed the sympathy and understanding of his superior. Fiszel clearly remembers wondering how the Germans thought it would be possible for the prisoners to build a complete roadway with two lanes in each direction without the aid of diggers and concrete-mixing equipment and heavy transporters. He was soon to discover that that which he feared would be the shape of things to come.

Everything was going to be done with manual labour. Men would surely die with the effort that would be needed, for they would not be sustained by a regular diet and the vitamins that would surely be necessary for their survival.

It was only four days later, as he lay in his bunk exhausted, in dire physical pain from the devastating effects of hunger, when the first of his cabin mates died. In some way this event stirred Fiszel into action. No longer caring whether he lived or died, his morale and well-being having been reduced to an almost intolerable level in less than a week, he determined to find food whatever the risk. Spurred on by mindless adversity, he ventured to the perimeter one black moonless night to dig the first few inches of a hole under the fence. Each night for a week, his strength ebbing from his body at an alarming rate, his resolve to survive diminishing until he found himself begging for release, even if it meant suffering the same fate of his friend Josef, he diligently dug deeper until he found that he could actually crawl under the fence and out into the surrounding open field. It was most strange, for while he spent the days labouring and begging for death, by nightfall the resolve to survive and find the food he needed returned. He explains.

"It was the beginning of the madness that would gradually take over my soul, rendering me devoid of feeling for other humans, for myself, for my almost forgotten family, for suffering and for death. Only the desire to fill my belly kept me going."

Fortunately, there were no search lights, although the night guards wandered around seemingly aimlessly, likely at any time to come upon the errant boy. His luck held. When the hole was completed and successfully camouflaged, with bated breath he stole out of the camp and trudged the three kilometres to the nearest village. Until this day he cannot name the place, and wonders whether he ever really did know the name of the village that was to provide him with a life-line. At many of the first houses he called on the door was slammed in his face as, still in civilian clothes, he begged for a piece of bread.

Occasionally, he would strike it lucky and be given a bag of goodies, after which the door was stealthily closed before a word was uttered. There was one hotel in the village. Not exactly a hotel, more a workers' doss-house. But it was there that he found his greatest fortune, for one night he crept down the alleyway behind the hotel and just as he was lifting the lid to the dustbin, one of the junior kitchen staff come out of the rear door. His first reaction was to run, but the man smiled. He was about Fiszel's age. Saying nothing, the young man offered the small sack of leftovers to Fiszel. Peering inside, Fiszel could see fish bones, and pieces of crust, and remnants of other such delicacies. Eagerly and greedily he stuffed what he could into his pockets, boot-tops, socks, and under his flat cap, then hurried away to return to the camp. He anticipated a warm welcome as he unloaded his prize and shared it with his billet mates. Instead he was berated by Chaim who nevertheless partook of the feast. Weeks passed with Fiszel and the kitchen porter meeting regularly at a pre-arranged time, but Fiszel knew that sooner or later he would be caught. Although he had learned that the guards did not always arrive at a certain point at the perimeter fence at a given time, in general their movements were much more regular than he at first assumed them to be. He had been lucky. Chaim continued to berate him and even threatened to expose his secret nocturnal adventures, but in reality he ate the food with greater relish than he would get from reporting his friend to the authority. On one particular night, some five months after his arrival, he crept under his secret opening to discover that two other men, inmates, whom he did not know, had been at his escape route just before him, for he could see their images disappearing at some speed across the open field. He considered aborting his mission. They were careless even in their attempts to remain oblivious to the outward gaze of any of the guards, for they were running in crouched position instead of crawling the 200 metres to where they would find cover. Hunger and youthful adventurousness got the better of him and, motivated by the fact that the kitchen porter would be waiting for him by prearrangement, he crawled along the wet autumn grass to his first destination. When he arrived at the hotel rear yard, the two inmates were handing the kitchen porter something, probably money, and carrying away the bag that was meant for him. The porter looked at the approaching figure and ran back inside. Disappointed and furious, Fiszel determined not to return to the camp empty of hand. He began knocking on house doors again, as he had when he first started the escapade, only to be greeted at the first one by a grotesque resident of about 30 who punched him fiercely on his nose and slammed the door in his face. Fiszel remembers that the night was not spent entirely in vain, as a number of people at further houses were more receptive to his requests, and the fact that he was nursing a bleeding nose and a bruised eye, seemed to encourage their sympathy. When he returned he found the atmosphere in the billet was not the usual one of expectancy and joy for his safe return.

"You are in deep trouble, Fiszel. The night guard came for an inspection and has ordered me to take you to the office when you return," explained Chaim.

In retrospect, Fiszel can clearly recall the fear at that moment. The tears welled up in his eyes as he faced certain death at the hands of his ruthless captors. He knew that he would soon be dead, and that he would die in pain of such a nature that the nauseousness he constantly felt in his stomach, the sheer physical emptiness of his under-nourishment, would seem as nothing by comparison. Chaim accompanied him to the office.

The clarity of recall of the following events was as expected. "No man would ever forget that night for as long as he lived," Fiszel told me, with venom in his voice.

After some prolonged questioning, during which he was beaten several times with rifle butt and truncheon, he was ordered to remove his trousers. He waited, naked from the waist down. The S.S. officers poked at his circumcised digit. A Wehrmacht guard entered with a large basin that had been filled with freezing water and in which several lumps of ice floated innocently. Fiszel was ordered to sit in the water for about five minutes until his posterior became unbearably numb. Then he was lifted out and hoisted over a wooden chair, face down. One! Two! Three! Four! Lash upon lash of a multi-studded leather whip rained down upon him. He remembers feeling one of the guards lifting his shirt so that his back was exposed, just before he passed out.

To this day he still has the weals of his beating ingrained across his spine.

The next thing that he remembered was being tied to a post and hauled upward so that his toes barely touched the ground. His arms were stretched above him, tied together by a leather thong, and pinned to the post by handcuffs. The excruciating pain took him in and out of consciousness throughout the night. On one occasion he remembered looking across the yard and seeing the two prisoners who had paid the hotel boy for his victuals. Both their heads were bowed, while their feet dangled beneath them, just touching the frosty ground. At some point in the freezing night he remembers that the droppings from his nose froze to his skin. Each time he awoke, the pain sent him reluctantly but welcomingly back into oblivion. On one occasion during that long and dreadful night, Fiszel recalls that a warm sponge or cloth was wiped across his face for just a few moments. Later it happened again. Then again. It seemed that at intervals of every hour the ice was being cleared from his pain-wracked face and body. He was still naked below the waist. The man who was tending him wiped his genitals and gently held the cloth to his swollen, aching, stinging back. Suddenly, it was light. Two German guards were cutting him down, along with the other two. They were dead. Fiszel Lisner had survived!

Without the extras of food the whole billet began to suffer. Extraordinarily, and for the only time that he can remember this happening, many others in the camp shared morsels of their meagre allowance with him in an attempt to demonstrate their respect, appreciation and their sympathy.

He was not allowed any time to recover and was ordered to return to the building site immediately. But with the limited authority vested in him, Chaim managed to give Fiszel the lightest of all the tasks under his control. It was then that Fiszel found out that Chaim was the one who stole into the night to wash and bathe him. It was Chaim who had kept him alive.

The pains of starvation grew again and became ever more unbearable as Fiszel worked with his shovel. He was never allowed to wash his clothes so they all became grimy and dirty as a result of the work he was doing. Recovered now somewhat from his terrible ordeal, he began once again to steal into the night to find further supplies of food. I asked him whether he was scared. If he was caught this time it would certainly mean a public hanging for not only himself, but an additional six or seven fellow prisoners chosen at random.

"I was so desperately hungry that even my hair was beginning to turn white and my beard had ceased to grow," he told me.

"However well you write the account of these events, you will never be able to explain the incredible pain of starvation. Only the need for food drove me on and kept me alive. How strange it all seems, for I wanted to die. If I did, I wouldn't need the food, would I? And if I ate, I would live longer. It is, how do you say it, a conflict of needs."

In January 1941, shortly after Fiszel's 17th birthday, three men were caught in the village by Wehrmacht guards out for an evening stroll. The prisoners, now supplemented by further arrivals to replace those who had died, were marshalled into the yard and forced to watch as the three men, plus three more chosen at random, were hanged in front of them. Fiszel distinctly remembers the S.S. officer gazing for a long time at him as he wandered along the ranks of men, choosing the three who would join their unfortunate inmates on the gallows.

"Even though I wanted death, I was filled with the greatest of fear. A fear unimaginable to anyone not there, not standing in that line." The S.S. officer smiled knowingly, and passed on.

Once again Fiszel had escaped the long arm of death!

The routine of work, parade, sleep, work, parade, sleep, continued as many of the Jewish prisoners began contracting serious diseases. Lice were on everyone's bodies and their incessant, almost Dracula-like demand for skin and blood became one of the major problems Fiszel had to deal with. Only the continual starvation and the indescribable pain it caused were more prominent in the daily suffering and anguish that was his existence. Malnutrition, typhoid, raging impetigo, dysentery and dehydration were rampant, and daily deaths became of such magnitude that a truck began calling each morning at six to clear away the corpses of once healthy young men. Fiszel himself caught a mild dose of typhoid. Dysentery was less of a problem for he was supplementing his diet with what he could beg, steal or trade, until there was nothing left to offer for a morsel of bread.

By October 1941, the camp had been almost entirely reinforced by further transports of Jews, most of the original ones having died in varying degrees of tragic circumstances.

Some, most, died of loss of weight caused by an absence of resistance to illness. Many however were beaten to death, some hung for the most minor misdemeanours, and others shot, mainly for trying to find their way out of the camp, or for stealing supplies. After another painfully laborious day during that October, Fiszel returned from the building site along with others, to be kept waiting in the yard somewhat longer than usual. Normally the count took maybe half an hour and then each man was allowed to join the queue for his food allowance before crashing down on his bunk to beg for release from suffering and pain, hopeful that maybe one of the billet mates would die in the night before he had consumed his piece of bread. Incredibly, almost no conversation took place. The effect of 18 in that hell on earth had destroyed even the will to speak. From a healthy, rather chubby young man of around 175 pounds, Fiszel now weighed less than 100 pounds. He needed no scales to tell him this.

The desperate, leg-weary, forlorn lines of men stood waiting, not knowing what treat was being prepared for them this time. It had been the case that when they were made to stand in line after the count for an extended period, it was usually because there was going to be more hangings, more shootings, or perhaps a new game!

Two S.S. accompanied by two Wehrmacht would take some men out of the line, at random and for no particular reason, and administer a severe beating. Truncheons, pick-axe handles, whips and rifle butts were used. Fiszel himself had been selected on two occasions, and he stood in line at this particular parade knowing that if they selected him again it would be for the last time.

He recalls that they had been standing at rigid attention, many collapsing to be left unaided and unattended, for maybe an hour and a half, when finally two very senior S.S. officers emerged, one holding a long piece of paper, like a scroll. He instructed the bearers of several names to form separate lines in front of the main ones, who were told to step back six paces. Those had fallen, those who were comatose, or dead, would remain where they lay.

Sometimes in tragedy a small comedy presents itself. There was no humour in Fiszel's life, but he recalls smiling to himself when the two officers, who obviously had come to the camp for this purpose, began reading out a number of names. Many were already dead! Some were lying on the ground at that very time either dead or dying. It appeared that for every five or six names called out, only one managed to step forward. The officers became perplexed and referred their problem to the Commandant who for the first and only time Fiszel can recall, became embarrassed and subservient in his manner.

"He'll soon be at the eastern front," Fiszel mused!

After some heated conversation, a further list of inmates was sent for and produced, and after referring to this, the senior officer shouted that all the men who had arrived on the first and second transport should step forward. It was how Fiszel discovered that, of the approximately 400 men who were the camp originals, 200 in each transport had been reduced to just 14. He was one of those. Chaim was another. A couple of the others he still recognised, but of all the men who had left Zdunska-Wola, only those few had survived. Chaim was ordered back into line and the additions, who now numbered around 80 or so, were ordered to pack up their belongings in readiness for transfer to another camp at five the next morning.

It was just after he had collected the soup and the bread that several trucks pulled into the camp. Fiszel stood back watching the poor unfortunates dismount, hungry, thirsty and dishevelled from their journey, as he had been.

Among them he recognised his first cousin Wolev, son of Luzer's brother, Yiddle. Their eyes met for just a fleeting moment. Wolev stared, barely recognising Fiszel. Suddenly, a guard shoved Wolev into the lines for registration and Fiszel, without emotion, feeling or care, returned to his billet to pack.

Poland's western demarcation line between itself and Germany was practically a straight line that ran from Swinoujscie in the north, where the coast is met by the Baltic, and Liberec in the south, which also divides the land between Poland, Germany and Czechoslovakia. The only position of variance from this straight line is about one third down from the northern tip, at the River Odra (Oder) just a few miles south. On the German side is the Town of Frankfurt-on-

Oder. It was there that one of the largest German industrial complexes had been established. An enormous barracks, plus many factories, a roadway, and a large paper mill, as well as a railway siding were among the many buildings that had been constructed or were in the process of being built. Jewish slaves were being brought into the area from all parts of Poland, Holland, Belgium and France in order to speed up the considerable activity as this was clearly going to be one of the major sites from where the German forces would receive supplies for the confrontation with Russia. It would also serve as a transit area for the forces of the Third Reich.

Already the two countries were at war, for Hitler had not upheld the terms of his agreement with Marshal Stalin and had invaded all of Poland instead of just the western area. It was to this camp that Fiszel was being sent when he climbed into the cattle wagon on the long train that was waiting for them and hundreds of others who were arriving on foot and in trucks from other camps. The 80 men from his camp were all piled tightly into one wagon and the sliding doors slammed and locked on them. Even before the train set off, the stench became unbearable. There was absolutely no air and no light. The men were standing shoulder to shoulder like it was a Wembley Cup Final and too many had been allowed into the stadium.

Some were sucking in what saliva they could muster from their dry bronchial tubes and spitting, for one of them had suggested that if they did this they would create an atmosphere of condensation which would produce oxygen. Others were just being sick and vomiting bile as the train made its way west across the border. All that day they travelled in the same direction.

When at dusk they arrived at Frankfurt-on-Oder, several of them were dead, but still remaining in the upright position, for there was no room for them to fall. Fiszel, still amongst the fittest and youngest, was ordered to help unload the many dead bodies. According to his strained memory, he thinks that about 18 died before they arrived and about a dozen more passed away on the journey to, or shortly after their arrival at, the new camp.

After the registration ritual he was ordered to the large building that appeared to have been a former theatre or meeting hall. Inside there were about a 100 bunks lining the wall and the passageways. Fiszel, being one of the first in line, claimed one for himself.

He was to be disappointed, for it soon became obvious that there were many more men than the number of bunks available. Skirmishes broke out, they were too weak to indulge in a real fight, as men tried to join others who had claimed separate sleeping accommodation. Suddenly there were two and three to each bunk. Fiszel was joined by a Warsaw Jew called Stanislos, a one-time miner whose large cheek bones pressed through his skin giving him an almost skeletal appearance.

I asked Fiszel whether he offered objections.

"I looked at this man, he looked at me, and I moved over against the wall. At least I had the inside and I couldn't then fall or be pushed out like many of the others. Stanislos was a big man. He said, 'Stanislos'. I said, 'Fiszel'. Nothing more was said. I had no interest in either talking or wishing to know his background. Nor did he. All we wanted was some food!"

It was morning before they were given the now customary piece of bread, and this time, the first day, a treat. They were allowed to half-fill their billies with ice-cold water. Fiszel told me.

"It is a strange world. Many things remain a blank in my mind. Many things will never come back to me, for if they did I would probably go out of my mind. Among the most vivid memories was that tin can of cold water. It was like, what? Nectar. Like a bottle of cold lager to a man who had just walked across the Arabian desert!" The camp at Frankfurt-on-Oder was as big as the Epcot Centre in Florida, or maybe to an Englishman the size of one of our Butlins. Except that this was no holiday!

There was chicken wire around the whole perimeter and the camp was divided into sections. There were several halls like the one in which Fiszel was billeted and an inner ring of smaller billets only slightly larger than the eight berths he had recently left. All in all he remembers that there were around 2,000 workers on the sight. At the rear of his particular hall was the German civilian changing rooms and showers, with many lockers used by engineers and site foremen, plus the canteen which they attended for their midday meal. Outside the massive areas of construction could be seen, with the enormous paper mill alongside the railway track.

Later he was to discover that the carriages were being used as store rooms for the enormous amount of vegetables that were needed for the non-slave labour that worked on the sight.

Initially, Fiszel was given the task of cleaning the rubble away from some of the building areas, but later he was transferred to hod carrying, a task that drained his energy as the unsympathetic supervisors and the even less sympathetic guards drove him unmercifully. At first he considered that the guards were less inclined towards beatings and unsolicited games with the Jews, but this was an illusion. He had been there for only one week when a group of guards burst into the hall and dragged about a dozen men out to the yard in front of the civilian canteen. For no greater reason than sport, they beat, punched and kicked the defenceless Jews until finally, humbled and bleeding profusely, battered and bewildered, the unfortunates were allowed to fall to the floor in a heap. Some others watched from the doorway. Most just turned over to sleep, thankful that they had not been selected. Rarely did anyone go to their rescue. That night was the first of frequent attacks on his and other billets.

Many new cabins had been built shortly after his arrival to house the many Russians who had been captured and transported across Poland to help in the work. Some spoke of horrific acts that they had personally seen carried out by German troops. While in Poland they saw hundreds of women raped in the streets and subsequently murdered by rampaging occupation forces.

In every inspection of Russian P.O.W.'s, there were always some sorted out for torture and murder by shooting them in the back of their heads while they helplessly knelt down, usually after they had suffered a severe flogging. Only the toughest and fittest, most submissive, most silent, made it to the work camp. In another area French P.O.W.'s subjugated their inherent pride for the sole purpose of survival, but demonstrated their hatred of the Germans at every opportunity.

During 20 months on this site, before being moved for the Final Solution to Auschwitz, Fiszel all but lost his life, in his quest to find food at any cost, on two occasions.

The diet since that first day of the cold water was again one bowl of stinking, watery soup and one slice of bread. In addition to the now considered to be normal diseases, there was a plague of rats. They seemed as hungry as the inmates and it became commonplace for the inhabitants of his billet to be woken by the skirmish that occurred when one decided that, in the absence of food scraps, a boney fleshless Jew would do. Conversely, the rat was also being chased and sought for the delicacy of its own flesh, sometimes eaten raw, and occasionally cooked on a fire that was alight on the building site.

In desperation Fiszel began looking for ways to find some scraps. The civilian canteen dustbins seemed a good idea, but by the time he had thought of it a Mafia of other inmates had commandeered the bins every night. One night, with the bins duly guarded and the pangs of starvation becoming increasingly unbearable, he noticed that a small window had been left open high on the canteen building. In the darkness of night he crept out of the hall and made his way the short distance to the building. Search lights had been introduced but it was relatively easy to avoid their continuous span of the area. He climbed up and through the narrow aperture. He dropped down only to find he was in the locker area. He could hear voices coming from the room that was used as the eating hall, so any clandestine venture into there was out. Several lockers were open. In one he found a jacket. Inside the pocket was a watch. Sweating profusely, even though his body lacked liquid and the night was freezing, he grabbed the watch and climbed back out again, discontinuing a further search for something to eat. On a premonition he decided to bury the watch outside his hall instead of taking it inside with him. Fiszel knew that discovery would mean death by hanging, but it was the fear of reprisal to the others that made him extra cautious. He had no value for his life, in the broadest and widest context of long term survival. Only hunger! Only food! At any price! At any risk! Later that night the eerie whine of the siren rang out and a general alert was sounded, almost as if there had been a full-scale attempt to escape. All the 2,000 work force was marshalled into the yards and a prolonged search of billet and person was carried out. For four hours, until just before it was time for roll-call, the entire force of inmates was made to stand in silence while the search was conducted.

The watch had belonged to one of the most senior civil engineers on the site.

Nothing was found. Punishment for the offender plus ten inmates was threatened to be the most horrendous yet inflicted, if the culprit did not own up. Fiszel stood his ground. Somehow he felt safe among the thousands who were there, and of course there were several hundred civilians who were employed during the day but went to their homes at night, so anyone could have taken the bloody thing. For some unknown reason, after they were allowed back into their billets, it all went quiet and little more was said about the watch.

For every German effort there had to be some achievement!

Several men were tortured and some shot, as the searchers found many items of contraband among the meagre belongings of the inmates. Fiszel toyed with the idea of owning up to his crime, but decided that one more life, uselessly thrown away, would make little difference. Two days later Fiszel retrieved the watch and sold it to a French P.O.W. in return for his daily slice of bread. To Fiszel's certain knowledge the man died shortly afterwards from typhoid. He never found out whether or not the watch was retrieved from the man's belongings!

Then, in November 1942 Fiszel was moved to the paper mill. He was to work under a civilian charge-hand called Wolfgang Schmidt. Fiszel remembers the name well, for the man was the first to take a particular liking to the young Polish Jew, and because of this affection was to save Fiszel's life.

The wood carvings and sawdust and rubbish went through the mill to become reams of rough newspaper, and it was at this point that Wolfgang's department came into action.

Their task was to wait for the overhead cranes to transport the rough reams across the large factory room, and as they passed high above, to grab them off their hooks, guillotine each batch, weigh and record it, and then return it to an empty hook as they slowly passed by. At first Fiszel and one other manned two machines, one each, but later two more scales and guillotines were added so that they were each running two machines. The speed at which the bundles came across kept their arms continuously flailing above their heads, round, down to the guillotine, heave to the scale, and hoist back again to the hook. One passed above about every 15 seconds and with no break for repast, the days were unendurably long and hard. Fiszel thought he was going to die at any time unless he got some more food into him, for the work was draining every ounce of strength in his body. Sometimes, as he was even too tired to raise the small piece of bread to his lips to eat with the soup, he watched sublimely as an inmate would steal the bread from him. He had no resistance and no power to resist. Occasionally Stanislos would feed him as his eyes closed and the strength sapped out of his body. Sometimes he would fall asleep while he was actually attempting to eat. Finally, unconcerned with death, oblivious to danger, he left his workplace and ventured out to the store wagon. The siding was directly outside of the factory's rear exit.

One of the sliding doors was unlocked. No-one was around. He clambered up. Stole inside. The steam was coming out of the underside of the engine. He thought 'If I could steal some potatoes, I could lay them under the jet of steam and they would cook. Unbelievable. Jacket potatoes. Paradise.'

He stuffed as many as he could down his boots and down the inside of his work jacket, and down his trousers. Jumped off the wagon. Turned to run. Straight into the barrel of a rifle!

The guard asked what he was doing there. He mumbled an answer. "I came to look for something for the charge-hand, Wolfgang." "For potatoes?" No answer.

"Come, we see this Wolfgang. If he says that you are lying, Jude, I will have you hung for stealing. And five of your Jude mates!" Wolfgang saw the two of them coming towards him, Fiszel with one arm up behind him in a half-Nelson, stumbling in front of the guard. His quick realisation of what was happening alerted him immediately.

If the guard had asked him what was happening he might have been unable to substantiate Fiszel's story, but the young German private told him what Fiszel had said and then asked if it was true. Wolfgang said that he needed the potatoes because he had had no time to send his staff for lunch, and he had decided to give them some potatoes to take home with them in lieu of the uneaten meal, and that was why Fiszel was in the rail carriage. He had sent him there.

With a cuff behind the ear and a warning to be more careful next time, the guard pushed Fiszel away and returned to his duty. Fiszel says that he will never forget the incident or the kindly charge-hand. If he is alive today, then I am instructed to offer Fiszel's eternal thanks.

On an evening in May 1943, almost three years after his first introduction into slavery, a Wehrmacht corporal called in to the hall and approached Fiszel.

"Tomorrow you gather your belongings. You are being moved. You are going to a camp in your own country. Auschwitz. You are going to be gassed, Jude."

Fiszel thought that the idiot was just trying to frighten him. PEOPLE DON'T GAS PEOPLE, DO THEY?

A MAN DEPRIVED

CHAPTER 5

AUSCHWITZ

In every region of Europe occupied by the Nazis, the Jews were being hunted, humiliated, tortured and murdered. It was the most horrific, mindless, Satanic period of unquestionable evil the modern world has ever known!

No city, village, town, farm, house, shop, factory or office escaped the long arm of investigative scrutiny by the S.S. and the hated Gestapo. The enormous costs of lengthy investigation, enquiry, interrogation and execution were ignored in the fanatical pursuit to rid the earth of the innocent semites. Massacres took place in every land, from the far northern reaches of the Scandinavian countries, across into Poland, Lithuania, Romania, west to France, the Benelux countries, and even inside the Soviet Socialist Republic. In one city alone, Amsterdam, the Jewish population had been reduced from an original 80,000 to a mere 5,000. The scourge of the Jews by the Nazis knew no boundaries. Concentration camps, slave labour enclaves, 'medical test' centres for genetic experimentation, and death camps were set up wherever possible, but the orgy of human barbarism, hatred, atrocity and collective extermination was to be maximised in what started as a relatively small complex in the southern region of Silesia. A place commonly known by the name of the nearby town of Auschwitz.

Auschwitz was not just one centre situated inside one expanse of electrified wire. Not just one unit of extermination centres or mass underground grave yards. It was like a new town, sprawling across acres of land, filled with inhospitable shacks, where men lived and died from every type of sickness and neglect and from barbaric inhumanities.

There was also a female complex, separated from the male one, where sexual depravation was more the norm than the exception. Jewish women, young and aged, were being used for every type of experiment, for the gratification of hundreds of soldiers, and for genetic examination, nearly always without the aid of any form of anaesthetic. Virulent disease, sickness from neglect and starvation, was rampant. If a Jewish woman caught one of the more degenerating sexual diseases, she was removed from the group of 'hostesses' on offer and usually tortured before being put to an unmerciful death.

Under the name of its full title of Auschwitz-Birkenau, the first unit Auschwitz I was established on 27 April 1940, initially for the concentration of Polish political prisoners who were to be put to work in the large synthetic rubber and chemical factory controlled by the massive IG Farben group.

The town itself had been conspicuous by its insignificance when it was part of the Austro- Hungarian Empire. Known only as a junction on the Vienna to Cracow railway, with a branch line to Breslau, it continued its uninteresting life until Heinrich Himmler decided that it would make a good site for his ambitious plans to concentrate the benefits of a slave labour force from among the civilian prisoners captured by the armies of the Third Reich, and a particularly fine place for his evil futuristic extermination process.

To head this miserable, sadistical enterprise came S.S. Commandant Hauptsturmfuhrer Rudolf Franz Hoess.

Rudolph was the third son of the Baden-Baden based Hoess family, who joined the Munich Workers Party after a short stint in the army during the First World War. Born in 1900, he was just 18 when the hostilities came to their ignominious end. When the local intelligence inspector-cum- propagandist, Adolf Hitler, whose job it was to investigate the Workers' Party for political subversion, joined the MWP and later became its senior orator and leader, Rudolph found the cause unto which he could lend his undoubted talents for organisation and methods. His unique talents and undying devotion to the cause helped him quickly rise in the ranks beside his leader, and Hoess enthusiastically joined with his mentor in that man's attempt to overthrow the Weimar Republic government based in Berlin during the Munich Putsch in 1923. However the success that they dreamed of was not to be, and along with Adolf, Hoess was tried and incarcerated for five years (Hitler's sentence was only ten months). In 1928 he was released and quickly rejoined the Fascists, and shared in the growing fame of his gregarious, idealistic compatriot.

After Hitler's accession to the most senior political mantle in Germany in 1933, was made an officer of the S.S. and in 1934 a senior administrator of the newly established concentration camp, Dachau.

Following Germany's secondment of 10,000 square miles of Czechoslovakia, and attack on Poland in September 1939, Rudolf was sent as the most senior officer to Auschwitz. There he was to order special chambers for extermination, crematoria and laboratory equipment. He called for tenders and finally settled on two gas chambers, to be known as Bunkers 1 and 2, made by the German Armaments Incorporated company, a firm controlled and financed by the Third Reich. A specially tall chimney would be required for the furnaces, and this was designed and constructed by Messrs. Topf and Coy of Erfurt. The five furnaces were very modern and could accommodate 2,000 bodies every 12 hours, fitted as they were with three doors at each oven. The tender was won by the company because the furnaces were designed to use the 'body fat' of the dead as their major fuel. Now for the implements of murder! Providing the doors to the bunkers were of metal, with solid rubber surrounds, it was agreed that the commercial pesticide, Zyklon-B, supplied in tins by the German Vermin Combating Organisation, would be the most favourable. As each tin opened, pellets of the lethal gas would be shaken out and would then explode into the chamber and automatically become hydrogen-cyanideprussic acid. The Badeanstallen (bathhouses), the Leichen-kellers (corpse cellars) and the Einascherungsofen (the cremation ovens), were fitted. The tall chimney was built. Everything was in order for the evil plan to commence.

On 14 June1940, the first band of Polish political prisoners was taken to the new camp Auschwitz 1.

In October 1941, located near the village of Brzezinka, came Auschwitz 2, probably the worst of the three camps that were to be established, for it was for very short term prisoners who were nearly almost entirely European Jews. This camp was known as Birkenau. The exterminations had begun!

In a meeting in Berlin with Himmler, Goebels, Goering and the Fuhrer, it was agreed that production of essential materials needed to be stepped up for the ailing war effort. The Americans had been dragged into the European campaign after Pearl Harbour, and the Reichstaag knew that it would need enormous supplies of fuel, ammunition, rubber products and machine tools as well as vehicles and tanks.

Within the Silesian area were many establishments manufacturing these products plus a wealth of solid fuel in the mines.

In May 1942, Auschwitz 3 was established for the housing of a slave labour force that would include thousands of young Jewish women as well as able-bodied men.

A frantic programme of wooden hut production was implemented, and in weeks a camp that could house innumerable slaves was created near to the village of Dwory.

Commandant Hauptsturmfuhrer Hoess and his vile assistant,doctor Josef Mengele, called for further inmates from all parts of Europe. From France and Holland, and from the labour camps in Poland, and especially from the transit camp in Frankfurt-on-Oder.

It was to the newly constructed Auschwitz 3 that Fiszel found himself sent that cold, friendless autumn day in 1943.

(Note: In 1945 Rudolf Hoess was made overall Deputy Commander, Concentration Camps, Third Reich, directly under Heinrich Himmler)

After the war ended, the Hauptsturmfuhrer was captured and tried in Warsaw by the Polish authorities, and following unanimous conviction was taken back to Auschwitz.

AUSCHWITZ:
THE DEATH MARCHES AND FREEDOM

The train travelled almost the length of Poland from Frankfurt-on-Oder back into Fiszel's home country across the border to the south, and slowly pulled into the siding situated some three kilometres from the main Auschwitz complex. Once again, Fiszel had been incarcerated in a sealed cattle wagon with more people than the carriage could reasonably house. Once again he helped to unload the dead and dying from the foul smelling cell in which they had been transported. This time he was greeted by uniformed Jewish policemen, whose job it was to relieve the new arrivals of their belongings and to stack up the many suitcases, clothes and footwear that they carried and discard onto an ever increasing mound of similar possessions. The task of unloading smelly, three-day old corpses, some beginning to decompose, took more than an hour as there were hundreds being hauled down unceremoniously from their travelling coffins. The wagons needed defumigating and Fiszel could see a number of Jewish supervisors with mops and buckets climbing into the empty wagons. Several arrivees were commandeered to help clean out the mounds of excreta and fill bins with the ankle deep urine. Slowly, these tasks completed, a long line, about six or eight deep, was formed along the entire length of the platform. As Fiszel sauntered with the others, humiliated, exhausted and totally defeated, he observed the piles of suitcases and clothing that were being loaded into trucks.

"It is difficult to remember height and width, but I do recall that the shoes which had been taken from many, not everyone, reached above my height and obscured the sky from my vision.

How would they ever sort them out, I thought to myself. I looked down at my feet. They would not want my shoes. What was left of them!''

For three kilometres the lines of bedraggled people silently tramped their way forward, aware of the many, many guards sporting submachine guns and rifles walking alongside. At one point Fiszel found himself lagging a little behind the party in front of him. He soon caught them up when he felt the force of a rifle butt in his back. Eventually they came to a pair of large open gates. Further forward was another set of similarly constructed wrought iron gates, and above these was a half arc-shaped board, upon which was written the words,

'Arbeit Macht Frei.'

Fiszel remembered what the guard had told him back at Frankfurt-on-Oder. 'You are going to be gassed.' It seemed that work did not make one free, as the sign said. It made one dead!

As the line slowed, Fiszel could see a party of about four leather-coated Gestapo ahead of him, surrounded by some S.S. and a few Wehrmacht soldiers.

"Perhaps about a dozen or so in all," he recalls. "They were directing the line of people. There seemed to be no reason why some were sent to the right and others to the left."

Eventually it was his turn to face the Gestapo man at the front of the small group.

"I was looking downwards, unable to look at his face. I had seen them many times before. Evil. Eyes that seemed to be full of madness. They were the true fanatics. He poked a black stick, like a sort of truncheon, under my chin and raised my head so that he could look into my eyes and I into his. My look was not one of hatred or disdain, just acceptance really. I cared for nothing.

"Left," he called. Fiszel slowly moved to his left, the man's right, conscious of the people who had been behind him, fighting to stay together as the man and the young woman were made to follow him, while their two children were dragged off into the other queue. One of the S.S. officers made an attempt to actually console the woman by telling her not to worry, the children were being taken to special showers. They would meet up soon. But the rumours! The woman fought bravely to stay with her children but a final rifle butt on the head soon persuaded her otherwise. Fiszel and her husband helped her up, but shortly down the line she was extracted from their grasp and taken off into a line of disappearing women.

Apart from the women who had opened doors to him when he went begging for food, this was the only time that he had encountered a female in close proximity during the entire three and a half years since his abduction from Zdunska-Wola.

Ambling along in silence, Fiszel soon came to another enormous pile of clothing. At that point he was ordered to strip down, along with all the others. He was by now devoid of any form of embarrassment. Naked, he was handed a small piece of cream-coloured soap and ushered into an enormous chamber which housed about 150 people. When the room was packed, not shoulder to shoulder as in the cattle wagon, but fairly closely together, and the doors closed, he felt the welcome thrust of warm water raining down on his head and body.

He had expected gas fumes!

The fear and acceptance of certain death left his soul as he allowed himself the luxury of washing his filthy torso. For ten minutes, his spirits soaring, he washed and scrubbed until his skin was pink.

"I knew for all the world that I was not going to die at that moment. We would not be washing ourselves if they were going to kill us."

The water sprays stopped and he was ordered out to the furthest end of the chamber and handed a grey towel. Everyone was instructed specifically to dry their heads well. Fiszel could see the barbers shearing everyone in sight of what hair they had on their heads. His turn came. He passed on to a series of tables at which a number of S.S. men were sitting. He gave them his name, age, home town, base from whence he had come. He watched as the man wrote a number by his name.

Prisoner number 142097.

He passed along the line slowly to await his turn. The hypodermic needle filled with a black indelible ink was pricked many times into his skin. That same number 142097, but this time the 'artist' added a small upside down triangle. A clear indication, Fiszel was later to discover, that it was an identification mark, telling everyone who wished to know it that he was a Jude!

Onwards he ambled to be ushered into a large room with an exit at the far end. All along one wall was a counter and behind this wooden racks filled with uniforms. The Jewish supervisor looked at him, said nothing, and pulled down a jacket and a pair of trousers from one of the racks and handed it to Fiszel. On the chest of the pale blue, grey-striped jacket was a yellow star. On leaving the building he again was stopped at a desk. There his registration was checked and he was ordered into one of the many lines that were being formed.

Slowly he marched for what he recalls was maybe one and a half kilometres until he came to an annexe of the main camp which was called Yavosnow.

From a builder's mate, hod carrier, and a paper mill cutter and packer, he was now to become a coal miner!

In his overcrowded billet he managed to find an empty space on one of the bunks shared by two others where he was handed a cup of watery soup and a slice of bread. It was the first food he had been given since he left Frankfurt-on-Oder three days previously. For three weeks, fed with the tasteless, insipid soup and mandatory slice of bread, only once each day, by the Polish prisoners, Fiszel and the new arrivees remained in confinement. The stench in the overcrowded billet was all-consuming and regularly men passed out for one reason or another. Although there were around 150 in there, many periods of silence prevailed as there was nothing to say, nothing to do. The continuous pain of starvation was everything. Once during this period, a group of soldiers came in. Their mouths were covered by masks because they could not stand the foul smell for even a few moments. Their purpose was to reduce the numbers by transferring those weakened and emaciated to the gas chambers to make room for new arrivals. On these occasions, which were to occur with frequency, a particular number of men were chosen at random. Selection appeared to be carried out based entirely on the degree of emaciation of the victim's body, or perhaps his face just didn't fit. There were no selection standards applied, as the guards, often quite young and of very junior rank, tapped the chosen men on their shoulders and ordered them to line up outside. They showed no emotion, no feeling. It was as if they were choosing some people for a day out, or a picnic, instead of for instant death!

At the end of three weeks, the period of quarantine over, the prisoners were ordered into the yard outside of the billets. All in all there were around five or six hundred men gathered for what they assumed was a roll-call.

What happened next is not for the reader who is weak of stomach, for it is the most sickening event about which I have ever had to write. I questioned Fiszel several times as to the validity of this story. He remained unmoving and therefore I accepted his account of the next hour in his life.

Fiszel explains.

"We were facing the brick office block. A few soldiers stood around disinterestedly, until a staff car arrived with three S.S. officers in it. I believe that one of them, the most senior, was the Commandant, Rudolf Hoess. Out of the barrack building came several more guards and a couple or so more S.S. men. One of those opened a scroll of paper after speaking reverently to the officers in the staff car. They dismounted, but said nothing. There were now about twenty soldiers of various rank facing us with rifles or sub-machine guns pointed in our direction. Suddenly, many of us turned as we heard the click of a floor-mounted machine gun manned by two soldiers kneeling behind it. I believed at that time that I had only seconds to live. I could hear several of my fellow prisoners chanting quietly beneath their breath.

'Shema Yisroel, Adonoi Elohano, Adonoi Erchod. Hear me o Israel, The Lord our God is one'

The one with the scroll began to read in German the instructions for good behaviour and the terms under which we could expect to survive just a little longer. The officers, Rudolf and his two henchmen, continued to stand in silence, observing, a nothingness in their eyes. They just stared at us as if we were foul-smelling animals, which we were. At least to them. We had no dignity. We had no pride. We were chattels for them to do with as they wished. The frantically read discourse, accompanied by the now commonplace frenetic gesticulation, at its end, Rudolf and his two men climbed back into the staff car and drove off. We were ordered to turn to face the side, a small clearing between the blocks. The machine gun and the rifles were still aimed in our direction. In front of us now was a line of cabins with no doors. Each had a sort of sawn-off petrol drum mounted on two rows of bricks. They stood about eight or ten inches off the ground. Two very young guards came among us. One looked at me, passed by. Six men were chosen. As soon as they had made their way to the front, they were battered about their heads until they lay peering upwards on the ground. They were stabbed in the testicles with the ends of rifle barrels until they inched forward and their faces were under the 'petrol drums'. They lay on their backs, their eyes staring up into the underside of the drums. Six Poles were produced, I don't remember where they came from. Probably the mess hall for the guards. One thing was for sure, they had been eating! Each lowered his trousers and commenced shitting into the drums. There was a large hole on the underside of each drum. The mounds of excreta began dropping onto the prostrate prisoners' faces. Then the guards stabbed them in their testicles again, so that their mouths flew open with the intense pain. The shit entered their mouths. After this disgraceful exercise was completed, the prostrate men, their faces covered in excreta, the sounds of their gagging nauseous to our stomachs, were prodded backwards and each one was made to eat the shit, before he received a bullet in the head. After that, a roll-call was taken and the prisoners given a final lecture on what they could expect if they disobeyed orders. Some of the guards were laughing. Then, we were allowed back into the billet."

The next morning Fiszel was awoken by a rifle barrel prodded into his stomach. Along with hundreds of others he marched, chained together by iron wrist cuffs, for about two kilometres until they reached a minehead. The mine was called the Pilsudzki Mine, named after one of the great political Marshals of Poland who died before the war started. The cuffs unlocked, they were then packed into a rickety wooden lift which slowly dropped for several hundred feet, until it reached a dark clearing, from which ran several three-foot high passages. Fiszel crawled on hands and knees along a tunnel. It was almost black inside. Eventually he came to a slightly more open area although the height of the tunnel did not increase by much. He was handed a pick by one of the Polish civilians who were to act as supervisors.

From the hour of seven in the morning, regardless of meteorological conditions on the ground, and regardless of bodily condition, until 12.30, Fiszel laboured in a crouched position to cut the rock-hard coal. There were hundreds of men spaced about four feet apart along each wall doing the same thing. Between the walls, in the arc-shaped tunnel, was a rail line and at 12.30 several wagons began rolling towards him. Men were shouting to stand aside, as the space between the walls and the central rail line was barely adequate, unless the miners pressed themselves against the walls. Some did not hear the warnings. The noise diminished their senses. Some of the new ones. On that first day three fell against the wagons. Many new to coal-mining were hit by flying shrapnel during the morning. Many were injured, some badly. Some fatally. There were no bandages, medicines, or drugs. Sympathetically, a few of the Poles produced handkerchiefs and strips of linen that they carried with them for the purpose.

Fiszel sat and watched the mayhem, with others less concerned. They had seen it many times before, particularly when there was an input of new men. The Polish civilians began to unravel packets of sandwiches and lunch boxes. These were the ones who lived outside the complex. The man next to Fiszel offered him one of his sandwiches. Fiszel remembers that it contained a sort of liverwurst. It was like manna from Heaven. He then understood how some had managed to remain alive for long periods. How they kept their strength. How they avoided the monthly gas chamber selections. At six the shift finished and he was allowed to stand naked under cold shower taps for five minutes. Then they were all chained together again and marched back to the billet, where they were given the customary soup and bread. His uniform was covered in black dust, but no clean ones were offered until the day he was to leave. The particular Pole who had shared his lunch box with Fiszel became a sort of friend. After that first day, the man's wife continuously packed a little extra for the young Jew who worked with her husband. When Fiszel was on a night shift, which was the only time he got a day off, there was another who brought him some additional morsels. It was enough for him to retain sufficient strength so that he avoided selection until the camp was evacuated in January 1945.

The months passed by. There were now two types of selection. The regular sifting one that meant a transfer to Auschwitz 2 and certain, instant death, and the 'sport' selection. This was when some of the guards became either drunk or bored and decided to have some fun with the slaves. Without warning they would burst into the billet and usher out the chosen unfortunates. Once in the yard they would beat and batter them until they became unconscious, after which they would leave them to either die or recover. Fiszel can remember being selected twice for one of these 'fun' evenings. The first time he received such an enormous blow from a rifle butt across his mouth that almost all of his teeth fell out. He lay on the ground, his mouth pouring blood, listening to the laughter of his young tormentor. The second time he was battered about the back and head, remembering nothing until he awoke from unconsciousness later that night. Someone had carried him inside once the guards had finished with him.

The war had turned badly for Germany. In June 1944 the Normandy landings meant the beginning of the end was in sight. Still, the Reichsfuhrer was determined to rid the country of the Jewish element. Gassing and disposals increased. Faster and faster the transports came to Auschwitz in order to achieve the final solution. But there were too many, and the Allies were coming! The Russians were moving across Poland, west, while the British and the French and the Americans had taken Paris and were heading for the Rhine areas. Many Germans knew that the end was near. They did not wish the Jews who remained in the camps to be found by the Russians.

At a meeting this time between Himmler, who was to be sent to command a force in a north western region of France, and Rudolf Hoess it was agreed that the Commandant should take command of all the concentration camps in Europe. He was to remain under the personal guidance of Himmler, but he would be in charge of the final attempt at total extermination. The Jews would be sent on 'Death Marches' across the land until they dropped from sheer exhaustion. Should they stumble along the way, then the accompanying guards were to shoot them in the back of the head. Were they to fall sick, or become a hindrance in any way, the guards would kill them immediately. Those who managed to survive might well end up being shot anyway!

Get those who were still walking to dig roadside graves and cover up the dead.

On 17 January an attempt was made to evacuate Auschwitz. With the Russians closing in, it is estimated that 28,000 were sent on 'Death Marches' before the Germans deserted the complex.

Rudolf Hoess by this time had mobilised hundreds of soldiers all over Europe to carry out his incredible orders and proceed with the final Jewish extermination before the Allies and Russians arrived. It was an impossible task.

Still, at Auschwitz, 7,650 people remained when the Russians finally broke through some ten days later, on 27 January.

Fiszel was on a march in the fiercest of winter conditions to a camp at Blechhammer, close to the river Oder, near the German border with Poland. Before he lined up with approximately 7,000 others, he was given a new uniform and one half of a loaf of bread.

For four days they marched slowly, painfully, many dropping by the wayside, many being shot along the road, stopping in fields or in barns at night. Fiszel himself found that his toes were freezing, and he began to limp badly. The ability to walk gradually deserted him and he knew that once again he was facing certain death. He made it to the first stopover but after Blechhammer, while resting in a barn, he explained to one of the others that his end was nigh, and that he could go no further. His toes were numb and the freezing conditions gave him no opportunity to recover. He would accept his fate.

"I told the man that if he made it back to Warsaw, from whence he came, after it was all over, to at least try to find my father or sisters and brother and tell them what had happened to me. I had seen too much, endured too much, suffered too greatly. My feet were like ice blocks, the pain excruciating with every step. I have no idea why I continued to try to walk. I didn't care one iota whether I lived or died."

The man would have none of it! He packed Fiszel's feet into what rags he could find, fed him with some corn kernels that were still in the barn, crushed some snow for a drink, after which he and another supported Fiszel until they reached their destination. By the time that they arrived, over 2,000 had died along the way, their bodies strewn by the side of the road in shallow graves.

On reflection and after I asked Fiszel why the men bothered to help him, he told me that their reasons were probably selfish. By holding him aloft, they were actually trying to retain some heat in their bodies, which would help them sustain themselves as well as keep him from the ultimate fate.

On further consideration, he recognises that the old word, 'Beshert', was in evidence once again!

At first some attempt was made to hide the hideous slaughter with mass burials, but this slowed progress, and eventually the numbers were too great so the German guards gave up the idea. Those who died were just left where they dropped, or shoved and kicked to the side of the road. Others who were still alive but too sick to continue, were carried to the side and unceremoniously delivered of a bullet in the back of their heads.

They stayed at Blechhammer for two days during which time Fiszel lost all remaining feeling in his foot. To this day several toes are still black and devoid of all feeling.

During the first night, he was woken by the sound of the engines of many trucks and vehicles. Watching through the billet window, he saw that all the guards were leaving. In the early hours the Auschwitzers and the many prisoners who were already at the camp when they had arrived that evening, ran into the yards shouting and calling and praying on their knees. Fiszel crawled along with them. Freedom! They raided the stores and like animals pulled at sacks of rice and grain and anything that they could lay their hands on. For the whole of that day people could be seen thrusting food into their mouths like rodents let loose in a cheese factory! Many became ill. A few actually choked themselves to death, while others died from consuming too much, for their digestive systems could not cope with the amounts they were stuffing into their shrivelled stomachs.

Then, in the late afternoon, the German trucks returned.

The inmates were distraught to see their captors arrive. They were quickly marshalled up and returned to the billets. The next day they continued their march, this time heading for Dachau, several hundred kilometres away, and one of the most notorious of the concentration camps.

Dachau was the first. A concentration camp located in Bavaria, in the south eastern corner of western Germany, on the Amper River, 16 kilometres north west of Munich, especially commandeered from an old munitions factory on 10 March 1933, only five weeks after Hitler became Chancellor.

He placed the S.S. in charge of the nightmare that the camp was to become for more than 250,000 Jews. During the years of the war, 150 branches were set up in Bavaria and across the border in Austria, all under the name of Dachau. Like Auschwitz it became a series of annexes and complexes under ruthless administration. Over 132,000 people died there mainly from abuse, physical decline and sickness. The gas chambers that were purchased for the camp were installed but never used. They had devised many and various methods of extermination. Not least by way of medical examination. Dachau was the first centre for experimental investigation by doctors and scientists to be set up by the Reich. The ruthless doctors specialised in finding out the effect of specific temperature changes upon warm flesh, freezing of live beings and the effect of varying atmospheric pressures on the mind and body.

In one specific operation, and for some reason known only to the administrators, many Jews were fed only sea water. Later the Allies were told that it was another form of examination to discover the effect on a human being's mind when this was the only diet. In another 'test', many Jews were to be infected with malaria so that doctors could examine the effectiveness of new drugs.

For many days Fiszel, along with several thousand others, falteringly trudged on. By the time they reached their next destination the original 7,000 was down to about 2,000, although the contingent was increased by the prisoners who had already been at Blechhammer and Dachau. It was at Dachau that they were allowed a further half a loaf. There were no people to make soup. The snow acted as their liquid refreshment.

The guards were now in a quandary, and many went AWOL, but there were still sufficient to carry out Hoess's plan, but it seemed that they were not sure of what they were supposed to be doing. Vehicles came and went, until the third morning when once again the prisoners were assembled together. They were on their way from Dachau to Gross-Rosen, another camp, this time situated in German-occupied Czechoslovakia.

Were they walking in a U-shaped arc, for they had already passed nearby to Gross-Rosen, when they left Auschwitz to walk to Dachau via Blechhammer? Following the marches on a map and joining the dots together, a 'return arrow' can be traced, which more than vaguely resembles the shape of the borders of current day Israel!

Gross-Rosen. A small Nazi concentration camp situated some 60 kilometres South of Legnica, near the town of Striegau. Now known as Strzegom, Poland. As in Auschwitz, they had their own gas ovens. These were installed in November/December 1941 and were being used for the extermination of those Jews transferred from Dachau. Was this the camp where Fiszel would reach his final resting place, and the relief he sought? After just one night at this latest commune, the marchers were put into cattle wagons for the short journey to a further camp, this time in northern Bohemia, not far from Prague, the capital of Czechoslovakia, known as Theresienstadt.

It was no accident that the prisoners were transported to this place, for a special scheme had been devised for the final extermination. Fiszel had been on the road for 34 days, and had walked at the rate of about 24 kilometres each day.

I brought Fiszel's memory into question at this point, but after examining the map and measuring the distances and the probable route taken, 24 kilometres each day seems accurate.

He had marched on infected feet, dressed only in the thin uniform of an Auschwitz slave, sustained by the cupboard raid at Blechhammer, and what scraps could be dug up in the fields as they lay at night, or that which could be found in the barns of deserted farm houses, for a distance of over 800 kilometres.

Theresienstadt Czech Terezin, opened in November 1941 to be used as a walled ghetto. In July 1942 the entire non-Jewish population of 3,700 Czechs was evacuated to other locations, mainly in the capital, to make way for 53,004 Austrian, Polish, German and later Danish and Dutch Jews. During its period of occupation, 33,500 Jews would die from starvation, disease, neglect and overcrowding. 88,000 Jews would be sent to Auschwitz for extermination.

It was now February 1945.

In Theresienstadt the Germans had a munitions factory. For three months Fiszel made bullets. Loading the powder into the small arrow-shaped metal containers, he slaved away, only this time there was even less bread and sometimes no soup. He was beaten frequently, and once a blow on the arm caused an enormous abscess to form on his elbow and there were signs that he might lose the arm from gangrene. Somehow, with care and a little help from whoever, and even with the absence of any drugs, the arm healed by itself. On another occasion his ankle was fractured from a blow with the butt of a rifle. The soldier decided that Fiszel was not walking fast enough.

By early May the Russians had broken through nearly all the German defences in Poland and the enemy found themselves in total retreat.

At Theresienstadt, many of the Germans deserted. But others came to replace them. Still the prisoners were dying from malnutrition, typhus, weakness and ill treatment. Many were at the very end of their tether, unable to keep mind and body together. Would they have mustered sufficient strength to stay alive if they had known that it was nearly all over?

Thousands never made it to 8 May 1945, when the final remnants of the German army deserted their barracks, never to return.

Unbeknown to Fiszel, I have discovered that the German officers in Theresienstadt, following instructions that appear to have come from Hoess, had arranged a mass execution of the inmates for the next day, 9 May.

In the writings of Rabbi Leo Baeck, probably the greatest Jew to survive the Holocaust, it was discovered that he, after many years of defiance, was to be shot on that day along with hundreds of others.

Fiszel Lisner had escaped the Final Solution once again, and until he reads this, he would not know that this would be one more occasion when he, somehow, some way, by the grace of God, was to defy death and remain on this earth, so that he could tell us his story.

The Russians arrived to declare that everything was over.

Almost five years to the day he was abducted by the Nazis to the first labour camp on the Polish border, Fiszel Lisner was finally, indisputably free!

His body was emaciated so that no-one who had known him would recognise the podgy youngster who worked alongside Luzer in those distant days back in Zdunska-Wola.

He had been deprived of the wonderful years when a young man discovers the opposite sex, and sex itself; and the joy of courtship, of love, of education and of communication. He had been deprived of food, and sustenance, and family; of all joy and the frequent happiness that forms part of everyone's life; and of all those things that we take for granted.

Perhaps, after reading this account, we may not accept everything in this life so readily as our divine right.

He had suffered as almost no other before him. He had defied death on too many occasions to describe in this biography. He had cheated and stolen and become a solitary human being, his mind only intent on finding food for his survival, when survival itself seemed not to matter.

He was not aware that only three others in his entire family of 48 had made it through the devastation. Brother, sisters, father, grand-father and grand-mother, uncles, aunts and cousins, had failed to survive the terrible inhuman injustices, purgatory and hatred of the Nazis of the Third Reich.

Fiszel was not to know until much later, that his father, Luzer, had been taken from the ghetto in Lodz on the final transport to be gassed at Auschwitz, while he was working down the mines at that very same camp.

Not for the love of another being. Not for the love of our country. Not for the love of our monarch, our president, our God, not for gain or for profit, not for fame or for personal gratification, not for work or for comfort, must we, the human race, yes you my readers, allow such atrocities to be inflicted upon other human beings, whatever their race or creed, ever again.

CHAPTER 7

THE JOYS OF FREEDOM

For those who were prostrate, waiting for death, a renewed feeling of well-being entered their souls, so that they found the strength to crawl. For those who were able to crawl, a renewed feeling of well-being entered their souls, so that they could manage to walk. For those who could still walk, a renewed feeling entered their souls so that they could now run. And for the most recent arrivals, who had suffered the least and who could therefore run, a feeling of well-being entered their souls so that they could jump and leap, high up to the sky, and praise their God. Men cried openly, producing the tears that would not have normally filled their eyes. Strangers hugged. Supervisors, Jewish policemen, informers, collaborators and ordinary prisoners were as one, as the Russians came, smiling, to declare that there was nothing left to fear, nothing more to suffer, no further humiliations, no further indignities. No more hangings and indiscriminate shootings. No more mass retributions for minor misdemeanours.

Some prisoners had been incarcerated for weeks, others for months, some for a couple of years.

Fiszel Lisner, for the whole duration.

But it was not, however, a time for deliberation. It was not even a time for revenge or retribution or recrimination. It was just a time to eat and feel free. Free as the wind. Free as a bird. Free as all human beings should ideally be.

On that first day, 9 May1945, a day that will remain in Fiszel's memory for the remainder of his life, only the feeling of freedom and the end to the unbearable pains of starvation were important.

No thought was given to those who had perished under the evil, tyrannical, maniacal Germans. No thought to those who had survived, to those who had escaped, or to whether brothers would find brothers, mothers would find children, wives would find husbands. Friends would find friends. The passage of time and the dehumanising effect of all that had gone before rendered Fiszel and his fellow survivors immune from the pain of others, the anguish of those who had suffered in similar circumstances. It mattered not that some, even then, would die very soon afterwards, for they were too far gone to save. It mattered not that some would remain crippled and infirmed for the remainder of their lives. It mattered not that the people who would be strong enough to throw off the effect of their experiences would go forward into life, scarred and tainted by the horrors that they had been forced to endure.

Only self was important. Food and freedom was all that mattered, as an individual attainment, a self congratulation, a self preservation, a self achievement.

Who could blame them? Each and everyone there in Theresienstadt and in other camps spread across Europe cared only that somehow, someway, maybe with some divine intervention, they had been chosen to survive.

Hundreds gathered in marauding gangs in the Theresienstadt camp to raid the kitchens and the store rooms in order to devour every particle, every morsel, every crumb of food that they could lay their hands on. It was then that Fiszel, as a member of one of these scavenging hordes, found the two frightened Wehrmacht soldiers, cowering in the canteen that had been used by the staff. Fiszel explains what happened next.

"There were about a dozen Russians with us. They had found boxes of rifles and small arms on one of our many raids into previously restricted areas. They had handed these out to anyone who still had the strength to hold one aloft. The gang was about 40 or 50 strong. We followed the Russians into the canteen. Behind the counter, sitting in crouched position, were these two guards. I have no idea how they came to be there. Maybe they had been too drunk to leave with the main party. More likely they had been into Prague or somewhere and returned after the others had left. Who knows? The Russian soldiers taunted them and grabbed them by the scruff of their necks and hauled them up. Then they beckoned us to follow them. I could see the two Germans quite clearly. They were both in their thirties. One was blonde, quite tall. The other about the same size and he was looking anything but Aryan with his dark eyes and brown hair. I followed the crowd into the communal showers. The Russians marched them into the middle of the floor. They were ordered to strip. Someone turned on the water. It was freezing cold and I saw them shivering. One, the blonde one I think, began crying and appealing to us. I stood back. I knew what was going to happen next. There was a certain feeling, a sort of atmosphere rising all around us. Suddenly the water was turned off and the mob moved in.

It was at this time that I became aware of some of our people standing on the security balcony. It was where the guards used to stand to watch over us. One among them, known to us as our unofficial leader, began shouting for us not to hurt the guards. Not to beat them up. I glanced up, and saw him waving frantically. He was distraught and was calling and shouting, imploring us to behave with dignity and not to inflict our wrath and anger on the two unfortunate Germans. I did not know the man's name. It is only since I have been telling my story that I now know that the man must have been Rabbi Leo Baeck. With sticks and rifle butts and revolver barrels they beat the two defenceless men to an absolute pulp. In less than five minutes they were turned into bloody, unrecognisable carcasses. Many cheered when it was all over."

"Were you one of those who hit out?" I asked, "You have nothing to fear. Nobody who reads this account of your life under the Nazis would blame you for anything that you did."

"I did not have a rifle or a hand gun. I wouldn't know what to do with one if I did! I swear that I only watched what was going on, but did not participate."

"What happened next?" I questioned.

"We left them there. I tell you. They were not even recognisable as human corpses, so battered were they. Who could blame anybody for it?"

After the revengeful murder the mob found several more store cupboards in the canteen and they disbanded into smaller groups in order to make up for the years of starvation. As in Blechhammer people ate and ate until they could consume no more. The Russians made no attempt at organisation, or control, allowing the inmates to scavenge and to hunt for further Germans, to plunder and to steal and to enjoy without recrimination or criticism their first day of freedom.

At this point I must make further mention of Rabbi Leo Baeck. This was a man who took Jewish children to England and returned to Poland, knowing that he would surely be arrested, tortured and incarcerated. This was a man who suffered incredible humiliation and unspeakable indignities for one of his high order. But this was a man who refused to submit to any of his tormentors' demands, and a man who found out how to deal with the Nazis. A man who against the odds survived it all to travel to Israel and to write classic accounts of that country and also of his experiences under the Third

Reich.

Between the years of 1939-1945 Rabbi Leo Baeck was a beacon of light in the evil storm of uncertainty.

The reason for this note is that he received unequivocal praise for preventing the survivors at Theresienstadt from harming the Germans who unaccountably remained at the camp after the main exodus. I questioned Fiszel about his story of the murder of the two guards, but he refuses to retract one iota of what he remembers. Reluctantly, I am forced to ask if this throws into doubt Rabbi Baeck's account of 9 May?

For the whole of that day all Fiszel can remember is eating. He stuffed every type of food that his gang found into his aching stomach until he nearly passed out. He was one among many. By the late afternoon practically everyone who he met was beginning to realise that maybe it was really true. Maybe they were really free and everything would soon be back to normal. What was normal? No one who was there on that eventful and wonderful day could possibly imagine what had happened. There would be no return to normality!

Many were still crying. People who had ignored each other for ages suddenly became friendly and warm. Men were sitting around in every area of the camp, particularly in those areas that had previously been out of bounds, eating, drinking, talking and praying. A Russian came over to where Fiszel's group was sitting on the ground forcing open several tins of meat to continue their feast. He handed them a number of rifles and pushed a revolver into Fiszel's hand. One among them who came from a region east of Warsaw and who spoke fluent Russian as well as his native Polish, asked whether some of them might go out into the nearby village. The Russian shrugged his shoulders and indicated that it was of no concern of his, and anyway they were free to do what they liked. In time, some semblance of organisation would come along and they would all be transported out of there and returned to wherever they wished to go. With trepidation, the fear of restricted movement not yet dormant or dead within their hearts, Fiszel and five of the newly formed gang walked into a nearby village. The streets were deserted. Many white flags flew out of upstairs windows. Not a Swastika was in sight! They entered a house that seemed deserted. Once inside they found a family of two adults, a young man of about 14, and two little girls, all cowering in one corner. The man fearfully stepped forward. He spoke in German. He was pleading and crying and begging the raiders to spare his family. He went to a drawer and pulled out notes. Reichmarks. Then he went to a cupboard and showed Fiszel and his mates some jewellery, among which were some watches and diamond rings. He handed them to Fiszel. Fiszel accepted it all and turned and ran out of the building followed by the others. The pattern was set! That same evening they raided several more dwellings, once entering a small block of apartments, where all the residents handed over, without demand, their valuables and belongings. Back at Theresienstadt they shared their booty. They dressed in the fine clothing they had been given and once again felt like human beings. The next day, Fiszel and his friends were given the freedom to roam around the local confectionery factory. He remembers eating so much chocolate that he became violently sick. For the whole of the following week, they continued to raid the local villages, some even going into Prague to do the same. Not on one single occasion did any of the residents resist or prevent the pilfering, many offering their valuables willingly in order to get rid of the marauding gangs. Many shops found that their stocks became vastly reduced when one or more of the gangs decided to raid. Foodstuffs were most popular. Clothing next. Then luxuries and jewellery. At the end of the week, Fiszel believes to this day that he was actually a millionaire, so much money and valuables had he collected. The gangs had broken up into twos and threes and his small group had filled their dormitory unit until it became difficult to find room to move. One slept on the floor, allowing his bunk to be stacked with the spoils of their plunder.

It was exactly later one week that Fiszel first felt the pains and the sweating and the rise in temperature. During that same night one of his roommates was forced to call for a Russian, who in turn sent for a military doctor, many of whom had arrived that week. He immediately diagnosed typhus and arranged for Fiszel to be taken to hospital in Prague.

For five weeks he lay in his comfortable bed, fighting the call to his Maker once more. But again he managed to beat the odds. Again Fiszel Lisner was not ready to give up on life on this Earth, whatever the adversity!

I was once staying with a friend, a famous football player and more famous manager. He told me that his mother had warned him before he left his home in Scotland to sign for his first club. 'Tommy, just remember when one door closes in your face, there is always another to come up and hit you in the head'

Could anything have been more true? Having suffered as much as any human being could have done, having defied death on numerous occasions, having been tortured and humiliated, beaten and starved, Fiszel now found that his God had deserted him once again, in only his first week of freedom in five years.

But it was not 'Beshert' that he should die. It was also not 'Beshert' that he should come out of his hell with spoils and riches, for after six weeks he returned to Theresienstadt to find that the others in his room had gone to their chosen destinations and taken their own and Fiszel's share of the booty with them.

There was order in the camp now, and he immediately was asked for his preferred destination, given rail tickets and some money, and allowed to board a train. He was going back home to Zdunska-Wola.

In truth he was far from impoverished, for when the doctors had moved him out to the hospital in Prague, they had taken much of his clothing and inside the pockets of several of the stolen jackets and trousers were many Reichmarks. In recollection he seems to think that it came to about £700 which was quite a small fortune in those days.

The train pulled in to the half-deserted town and with baggage in hand Fiszel made his way toward the square. He had gained weight, lost it during his illness, and then put it back on again quite speedily. Wherever he went people offered food and sustenance.

Even though the Russians had given him his train fare and some spending money, the ticket collector at the Theresienstadt station had taken none from him, happy to issue the ticket without charge. Suddenly, those who had taken orders willingly, sometimes with open enthusiasm, and who had developed their own levels of empathy towards the Nazi doctrines, became sympathetic and tolerant of the Jews who they had openly hated while under their invaders' regime. By now, the newspapers were disclosing the atrocities and there followed an enormous denial by individuals and groups of any kind of willing participation.

"Ah, how the worm turns!", Fiszel commented with poignant recollection of the station master's subservient manner.

The square was much as he remembered, but there was little else that was recognisable about the area of his former home. Number

28 was an open space and he could see the entire length of the narrow lane, with unobstructed view, where his father had led his horse and cart and which formerly backed onto the yards of his close neighbours. Where his bedroom used to be was a pile of rubble. He could just make out the foundations of the outside toilet in what used to be his yard.

"I gazed unbelievingly at the space. Where was everything? Where were the people? Some memories are of course obliterated from my mind, as you would expect, but the recollection of my feeling at that moment is another that has stayed with me ever since. I felt, how do you say it, desolate, alone, detached? I felt like I was in space with no meaning for time. It was as if I had taken one of those drugs that you read so much about these days, and I was somewhere different than on this planet. I don't know how to explain it."

I watched him wipe his eyes, and held back my own tears as I turned off the tape recorder and shared a silent cigarette with him. I looked at him. Saw the man. Saw the being. Observed him with awe and respect. I asked myself why one man should have to suffer such grief. We waited maybe a quarter of an hour. Mary served us some more coffee, our sixth cup. She smiled, knowingly. She had been his partner, his friend, his shoulder to cry on for more than 20 years, yet she had never heard his account of those times, before. I choked back my tears, made a joke about something inane, and tried to continue. I switched the tape machine back on.

After standing there for almost an hour, unmoving and still, the thoughts of the past racing through his troubled mind, Fiszel made his way into the square. The non-Jewish butcher's shop was open. There was little to display in the window but his father's friend, Tadec, was there. Fiszel tapped on the window. The man looked up.

'What do you want?' he called, but before Fiszel could reply, recognition came into the man's eyes. Fiszel watched him run outside and stop a yard away from where he was standing.

'Lisner? The boy FiFa?'

'Fiszel.'

'It is really you? My God, you are here, I cannot believe it! I am struck with dumbness. Let me look at you.'

The man waited a moment and then slowly took the 21 year-old boy into his arms, making no effort to quell the tears as they covered his fat cheeks. Unashamed, he sobbed until there were few tears left. Fiszel allowed himself to be hugged, and waited for the butcher's tears to subside.

'Come, come inside. There is no one here. Only me. The wife died three years ago. She was so hungry. She withered away like your mother. Do you remember my Svetlana? Such a big woman. She lived only to eat. When the rations dried up and your father stopped the deliveries she soon faded away."

'I remember.'

'Tell me what has happened to you? How long have you been gone? Four years? Five?'

'Five exactly. I left on the second transport. May, 1940. Where is everyone? Do you know what happened to my people?'

The man ushered Fiszel to a seat in the back of the shop, while he closed the front door to join him. Slowly he recounted a story of how one day, he had difficulty in remembering whether it was in 1941 or 1942, the Germans came swooping into the ghetto and gathered up all the children and some old people, although there were few of those by that time. How a couple of hours after that, a 'volksdeutch' (Polish-German) came into the shop for a sandwich.

The man was very depressed, and Tadek asked him what was bothering him, seeing how, being a German, he was living off the fat of the land, what there was of it!

He was one of the drivers and civilian helpers. The man explained how he had seen with his own eyes the soldiers take the children out of the trucks and dowse them with petrol before setting them alight.

Fiszel sat immobile, stunned at Tadek's revelation. His brother, Harman-Hertz. His sisters, Basza-Hendle, Toba-Chaja and little Sura-Faiga.

For some time, Fiszel cannot remember how long, he tried desperately to call upon the emotion that he should have expected, but somehow his own pain and suffering seemed to exclude the sorrow that he should have been feeling. Again the feeling of detachment. The immunity to feeling sorrow. He felt dead inside. Yes, he was truly sorry for the fate of his family, but it was as if it had happened to someone else, someone not of this earth, of his blood. Some people, terrestial and distant.

"And the others?"

"You were here when the kosher butcher was taken along with your grand-mother. Only Luzer remained. I can tell you that he was taken to the ghetto in Lodz. Your cousin Bella, she was there. She is in town. Like you, she survived. Also your friends. You remember the two sisters, Chaja and Udle and their brother Umerlaw, they too survived. They are here too."

"They escaped to Russia as soon as the Nazis arrived, I seem to remember. I bet they had it good.'

"I don't think so. They were locked up by the Soviets as soon as they arrived. Here, here, I give you their address. Better still, I take you. I have little trade. There is so little to sell."

The old man took Fiszel on his horse and cart to where cousin Bella was living. Unbeknown to either the butcher or to Fiszel at that time was the fact that another cousin, on his father's side, Charmel, son of Luzer's brother Yiddle, and brother to Wolev whom Fiszel had seen arrive at the first work camp, was living with Bella. Bella was a cousin on Fiszel's mother's side of the family. The reason that Charmel's association with Bella was being kept very quiet was that, contrary to the morality of those times and to the strict teachings of the Jewish faith, the two cousins were living together in sin. Remarkably, the sense of inpropriety had stayed with them through all that they had suffered. Fiszel was greeted warmly but not with the emotion that could be expected for a returning hero and one of only four survivors of the entire family. Bella was embarrassed, even with Fiszel, about her cohabitation. Later the cousins were to reintroduce him to the two sisters Chaja and Udle, who seemed more enthusiastic about the safe return of their good friend. They exchanged stories. The sisters had been incarcerated in a woman's prison just after the first German attack on Zdunska-Wola. Immediately, they had made their way east across Poland, through Warsaw, turned south to the River Bug, and entered the U.S.S.R. at Wlodawa. Once out of Poland they had turned north to Brest where they were then arrested. They had remained in prison during the whole period of the war. They were reluctant to recount the details of their period of incarceration. Suffice to say that they worked hard for little pay, were fed reasonably well, had to give in to the Russian soldiers who called there frequently, and reluctantly submitted to the demands of the powerful female guards.

The cousins had a different story to tell. Both were transported to the ghetto at Lodz with Luzer. When the final transport was arranged and the ghetto cleared of all its residents, Charmel and Bella were among those who managed to hide in camouflaged cellars, not believing the fables that the Germans told them about better times to come at more homely places with more food than they had been given for years. Even though the elders at the ghetto finally accepted the Nazis' lies, and encouraged everyone to follow them to 'paradise', both Bella and Charmel had been too suspicious of the tales to allow themselves to be taken with the others. It was then that Fiszel found out that Luzer had been taken to Auschwitz and gassed while Fiszel was at the camp digging coal.

For six weeks Fiszel lived with his cousins, but there was a great strain as his presence seemed to prevent them from expressing their love for each other in the accepted manner. One day, to his surprise, he returned from a visit to the sisters to find his belongings out in the street. Through the window he listened to Bella explain how they had decided they could no longer offer him a roof over his head. He listened to his cousin's reasoning. He cried and appealed to her better nature, but she was adamant he should find alternative accommodation.

"Where will I go?" he appealed. Her answer was to disappear into the room. Gathering his belongings, aware once again of the feeling of abandonment and loneliness which brought on a sense of detachment, he wandered back towards the house of Udle and Chaja. Fiszel crossed the square, where he could see some members of the Red Cross posting notices on a bill board outside the town hall. There were lists of other survivors from the town who were known to be alive in different parts of Europe. He wandered over. Old school chums. Old pals from the Heider. He spotted the names of five sisters of one of his best friends called Bendet. Bendet Lewkowicz. They were in a town near to Stockholm, Sweden. How they came to be there he had no idea, but he was pleased to find that they had all survived, although he was saddened by the fact that Bendet's name was not among them.

Purposefully he marched to the home of the two sisters, who offered him shelter willingly, but warned him that Umerlaw was in a camp in Germany and he was doing so well with black market trading that he would soon be calling to take the two girls back to his camp. The mission would be dangerous, for the Russian border guards were no longer allowing free passage into Germany. Fiszel accepted the situation but was mostly interested in writing to the five girls in Sweden, one of whom had been a special friend. He wondered whether old relationships could be renewed. Perhaps Bendet was indeed with them and the Red Cross had inadvertently left his name off of the list.

When Umerlaw arrived after Fiszel had been in residence for just two weeks, he reluctantly allowed Fiszel to travel with them to Germany.

"I think that he only agreed because I offered to pay my way with plenty on top."

Umerlaw would need much money to bribe the border guards if his mission was to be successful. It all went to plan. The Russians accepted Zlotis and Reichmarks and helped the foursome onto the train. The train stopped at Hanover. It was there that Umerlaw, older and more street wise than his friend, and perhaps feeling reluctant to allow Fiszel to muscle in on his operation, refused to take him any further.

Unceremoniously he took Fiszel's baggage and threw it all onto the platform. The train pulled out with Fiszel watching in despair, abandoned and alone once again.

In the brilliant September sunlight Fiszel stood outside the station not knowing exactly what to do next. Before Umerlaw had left he

had said, 'Go to Bergen-Belsen. There is a transit camp there.'
A motor cyclist came alongside him, standing close while putting on his leather gloves and helmet.
"How can I get to Bergen-Belsen?" Fiszel asked.
"I go past there. I will take you. Jump on the pillion!"
Fiszel laughed at this point in his story. He thinks that he was as frightened by the prospects of that pillion ride as when he was confronted by the S.S.
He was welcomed at the camp as many were still arriving from all over Europe. After being released, they too had made their weary way back to their former homes, only to find desolation and destruction, with many or all of their family missing.
Faced with loneliness and poverty, they were informed by whichever authority was in power to make their way to transit camps where they would be allowed to choose a final place almost anywhere in the world. Thousands upon thousands of lonely people were wandering around Europe aimlessly, each seeking a place to establish their roots and to start life again. Fiszel was no exception.
On entering the camp Fiszel was immediately shown to the building where registrations were taking place. There were more people than the clerks could cope with. Details were inserted into their books and papers. The clerk asked Fiszel his name, place of residence and birth date in quick succession. Fiszel was tired, lonely, hungry, and still recovering from all that had happened to him, including the hair-raising experience of the motorcycle ride. Somehow the number of his former home and his birth day became mixed up. The man had put down his date of birth as 2 January 1928 instead of 1924. It would have made Fiszel 17 years old, and he certainly looked older than that, but the man was so harassed he paid scant attention to the faces of the people registering with him. Before he

gave Fiszel a food voucher and directions to a sleeping place, he also enquired as to where Fiszel would eventually like to settle if it was possible to make the necessary arrangements. Fiszel considered Palestine. Then America. But he remembered he had relatives in England who had left Poland shortly after the end of the First World War. It was to there he indicated his wish.

Fiszel hated Bergen-Belsen after the comfort of living with his cousins and two friends. The place was austere and cold and offered little more than the basics required to survive. He had lived frugally for too long to have to contend with all that ever again. After only one night he made his way across country to a camp that had been recommended to him by one of the displaced persons in the transit camp. The camp to which he decided to aim for was in the American Zone, close to Frankfurt-on-Main in the historical region of Franconia, the west of Germany close to the Luxembourg border. It was there that Fiszel met and roomed with another old friend from Zdunska-Wola, Myer Sworzynski.

(At the time of writing this biography, Myer is still alive and has received Fiszel as a guest in his own home in New York.)

The room was quite large. Well furnished with comfortable beds, wardrobes and chests of drawers, it housed four young Polish Jews, all of whom had survived the years of atrocities. Except that Fiszel soon found out that on many occasions there had been as many as six persons in that room, two to each bed, as the handsome youngsters availed themselves of as many of the local females as would agree to midnight parties and to what that entailed. The camp, being in the American Zone, enjoyed supplies of everything from chewing gum to nylon stockings, all at extremely beneficial prices. There was much to attract the attention of the heavily-rationed young female residents of Frankfurt-on-Main!

It was shortly after his arrival that Fiszel had his first sexual encounter.

They had all gone to the cinema. When they came out, a group of girls was waiting around outside. One in particular seemed keen on the loud and happy young men who approached her, and soon, with the promise of Lucky Strike cigarettes, nylon stockings, wine and Double Bubble chewing gum, she joined the party in their room. Having four young men in one evening did not seem to bother her. It would be worth it for the spoils.

Fiszel was shaking and as nervous as he could ever remember as he watched his compatriot make love to the girl on one of the bunks. Soon it would be his turn. When the first boy had finished with the girl, he watched again as Myer did his bit for Polish/German relations. Now it was Fiszel's turn.

It was amusing to see Fiszel's embarrassment as he tried to explain to me what happened next. It may well be the promiscuous 1990s, but for Fiszel the subject of sex and women is still not one he can discuss freely, without some discomfort.

"Look Guy, I don't want you to say so much about it. She was the first woman I had ever seen naked, apart from my little sisters. It was only by watching the others that I really knew what was expected of me. You can understand. They were all waiting for me. Like any other boy I didn't openly admit I was still an innocent. Believe me, I was lucky to even get an erection after what I had been through. Do you think the Germans didn't put, what's that stuff, bromide or something in my soup and water. So, I went to this girl. I dropped my 'gutckers', I put it in, and well. Enough already. This isn't what the book is all about."

He really is a lovely man. I know I have said that before, but I was truly amused at his embarrassment.

"Would you both like me to leave? I'll make another coffee," said Mary.

"No it's okay Mary. What do you think happened, Guy?"

"I would think it was all over in a minute."

"Would you believe a second?"

We all laughed. There had been so few occasions when that very normal emotion had been present at these very distressing interviews. In accordance with the Jewish mind for trade and business, Fiszel was invited to join the small band of black marketers who inhabited his dorm, Apparently they had been at it since they had arrived some months previously. The American cigarettes that were being sold in Hamburg, within the British section, were greatly in demand, and by buying these at NAAFI prices and taking the train to the north, much money could be made. Not only that, but to return with the herrings that were eagerly devoured in Frankfurt, but were generally only obtainable at a good price in Hamburg, made the mission doubly worthwhile.

Coincidence is often stranger than fiction, and not for the first time was coincidence the cause of another momentous event in Fiszel's life. For it was to bring Fiszel together with his first true love and determine his future. What happened, firstly in a place called Neustadt-holstein and later in Frankfurt, would prompt his exodus to England.

The boys were making frequent trips to Hamburg and the many camps in the British Zone when they were invited to a get-together at a camp in Neustadt-holstein. There was a small crowd of both sexes there when Fiszel and Myer arrived. He immediately spotted Umerlaw and his two sister. The party was being held in the very camp to where Fiszel had originally intended to go before Umerlaw put him off the train at Hanover. But everything is 'Beshert', and

Fiszel soon became aware of why it was meant for him to be invited to this get-together. Umerlaw made his peace and, being the kind of man Fiszel is, he immediately forgave him. Later, after they had consumed some wine and exchanged experiences, a beautiful young girl, dark of hair and brow, trim of waist and with a large smiling mouth, but with sad eyes, came into the room to join them. Udle introduced her as their neighbour, Henya.

Fiszel was in love! He knew there and then that this was the girl he wanted to marry and settle down with. According to his story, Fiszel admits to being dumbstruck immediately he was introduced to her. Henya was another Polish survivor who had been saved by a much older man with whom she now lived. As soon as the two of them had been sent to Neustadt, the man turned into a monster. He treated the girl as a slave, demanding everything of her and giving nothing in return. He was 50 years old, while Henya was about the same age as Fiszel, 21. The girl was unhappy. Fiszel listened to her tale of woe and never left her side. During that whole evening he sympathised with her, and slowly the early pangs of desire turned to wonderment and love.

"I asked her why she stayed with the brute who was beating her at every opportunity. Why she just didn't leave him. She told me that she was grateful to him because of the risks he had taken to keep her safe and anyway, where would she go? She was the only surviving member of her family."

The next day she slipped away from her mentor and Fiszel took her to the cinema.

"I will always remember that day, for truly I have never stopped loving her. It was 17 April 1946. We had our photograph taken together."

That night he persuaded her to pack her things, what little she had, and accompany him and Myer back to their place in Frankfurt. To his surprise, Udle and Chaja told him how unhappy they were with their existence in their brother's home, and that they would like to go with them to the camp at Frankfurt-on-Main. Apparently, Umerlaw had a live-in girl friend and the sisters felt uncomfortable with her. Stealthily, when everyone was asleep, the party of Fiszel, Myer, Henya and the two sisters crept out of their lodgings and boarded a train back to Frankfurt. A room was found on the camp for the two girls, while Henya would stay with Fiszel. Of the three other room mates, only Myer did not have a regular girl friend staying with him.

Henya was shy. Even though she had lived as a concubine with her Svengali, with Fiszel it was very different. He, too, was bound by the moral teachings of his parents and what was acceptable before war came, when a couple in love were often chaperoned before they were married. The morality of those times and the respect Fiszel felt for the girl prevented a sexual union. Henya and Fiszel shared a bed, but never touched, and slept back to back, not once allowing their passion for each other to surface. Both were very conscious of the others in that room. Fiszel fully intended to marry Henya, but failed to tell her of his plans because firstly he needed to sort out their long term future.

On another business trip to the north, some weeks after Henya had joined him, Fiszel met another of Zdunska-Wola's survivors, and when they engaged in conversation about the five sisters of Bendet Lewkowicz still in Sweden, Fiszel learned that Bendet was astonishingly still alive and living in a camp near to Munich. Fiszel was elated and could not wait to return to Frankfurt so he could tell his love of the great news. A plan for their future was already forming in his mind. He had always felt an affinity with Bendet, so he would take Henya to Munich where they could start life together. Perhaps later, after they were married, he would take her to England to meet his relatives. The world was his oyster! The joy of being the one to inform Bendet that his five sisters were alive and the prospect of their forthcoming meeting made him happier than he had been since his days as a lad in Zdunska-Wola.

When he returned to the camp in Frankfurt, Henya had gone! One of the girls lived with a room mate told him that Henya had asked her why Fizel had never attempted to make love to her. Jokingly, her boy had replied that it was because the Germans had cut off Fiszel's penis. Henya had packed her belongings and fled their home immediately.

Fiszel was distraught.

He packed up his clothing and his ill-gotten gains and set out to return to Bergen-Belsen, firstly informing Bendet by telegram that he would meet him at that camp.

(Bendet is alive today and lives in Detroit and as often as either can afford it, the two men still see each other and telephone each other frequently.)

Only the reunion and the joy on Bendet's face when he found out that his sisters were alive helped to dispel the feeling of despair that had again entered Fiszel's soul. It was at this time that he wrote in desperation to his uncle Charlie and auntie Sylvia in England. He had always remembered their address. He received no reply until some time in July 1946, when a British soldier turned up at Bergen-Belsen asking for him. The man was the brother of Alf Rogers. Alf had married uncle Charlie's daughter. Charlie had seen his son-in-law's brother as a means for personal contact. The soldier informed Fiszel that uncle Charlie and aunty Sylvia were at that time on holiday in Spa in Belgium, and that if he wished, he had the means to smuggle Fiszel into that country. Without telling the authorities, Fiszel left the camp with the soldier. Later, they met with a Polish agent who it seems had devised a certain way of making much money by transporting misplaced people across restricted borders. He gave Fiszel a false passport which showed a man not very similar in features to Fiszel, but one who was a Belgian subject. Apparently the agent had managed to buy many such passports and was using them in the manner described.

The journey was easy, and although they had to dismount from the train as it slowed, by bribed pre-arrangement in a forest, their journey across the border was unimpaired. In Spa, Fiszel met his relatives, and just before their departure back to England, they took him to Brussels, where a distant cousin lived who agreed to allow him to live with them until permanent arrangements could be made.

For three months thereafter, uncle Charlie harassed the British Consul in Hanover, for the authorities thought that Fiszel was still at Bergen-Belsen, to grant the boy the necessary papers to come to England.

On Saturday 14 September 1946, Fiszel received a telephone call from uncle Charlie in England, advising him to return to Bergen-Belsen because the relevant papers were about to be issued, and the boat that was to bring him to England departed from Calais on the following Monday.

The journey that he had made from the camp to Spa three months previously was repeated in reverse, again accompanied by the well-reimbursed agent, but this time they walked in swirling winds and driving rain.

The speed of the call, the weather during the hours spent in the forest crossing the borders, the past, his lost love and the prospects of an unknown future in a strange and distant land, all contributed to make Fiszel enter Bergen-Belsen for the final time in total despair and disarray.

On Sunday 15 September, Fiszel Lisner, his incorrect papers in his hand, along with 12 others, boarded a train that took him out of Germany (to where he has never returned), back to Brussels, into France and on to Calais, where he left Europe for the first time. His spirit was low, his feeling of loneliness and detachment now a permanent part of his personality. But he would be starting a new life with a fresh beginning in his chosen land. A land of freedom.

CHAPTER 8

LEST WE FORGET

Political history has proven that ideology is often little more than the whim of expediency.

With regard to the political and economic upheaval in the world, and especially in Europe at the time of Hitler's accession to the Chancellorship in 1933, following the Wall Street crash in October 1929, and with regard to the power and wealth, both of a national and international consideration, it is difficult to assess what was expedient about the determination of the German leader to rid the country of its Jewish element. Certainly he needed a scapegoat.

The fluctuating fortunes of the German economy offered itself to the first man who could recognise the causes and rectify them at a stroke. In fact, they were more complex and more attributable to the Treaty of Versailles and the crippling reparation payments to France, Britain and Italy, than they ever were to a minority section of the population. When did the dictator begin to believe his own rhetoric?

At what point did a lowly Austrian infantry corporal begin to believe that he was the AntiChrist? Or maybe the Messiah himself? The one to cleanse the world. The one to inflict upon the peoples of other nations the Aryan persona as their master, even to the point of devising schemes that would make the new born clones of his image as a true member of the Teutonic race?

Did he suffer hallucinations while in captivity and during the writing of *Mein Kampf* in 1923? Did he hear the voice of the Devil, and come out of prison with uncontrollable feelings of grandeur? Was it the dedication of his followers and converts?

What possessed the ordinary peoples of greater Germany to follow the leader in his fanatical belief that his country could rule the world and cleanse it of the people who had trodden the ground since time immemorial? The people who had left Egypt long before the birth of Christ. The people who were scattered around the globe and who had resisted persecution, torture, slavery, and humiliation like no others but a people who had survived and would survive again. Ironically, the efforts of Adolf Hitler must surely have contributed to the agreement by the major powers to grant the Jews a permanent homeland in 1947, only two years after the end of the hostilities. When David Ben-Gurion declared Israel's independence in 1948, was he smiling within himself? Did he know? Was the price of liberation that which his people paid during the ultimate examination?

Perhaps we will never know what was in the Fuhrer's mind. What we do have are records and memorabilia, and accounts of the treachery and atrocities he inflicted.

While there is little doubt as to who were the main targets of the fascist doctrines during those horrendous years, it must not be thought that the Jews were the only ones to be tortured, murdered and gassed indiscriminately. Poles and Russians of non-semitic heritage were murdered in numbers even greater than the 6,000,000 Jews who did not return to their homes and who did not register their existence when the final curtain was brought down on the Fuhrer in that bunker in Berlin on 30 April 1945.

Hitler and his wife of one day, Eva Braun, according to history, committed suicide. The world was free when two days later all German resistance ceased and the European campaign came to an end.

It only required the Americans to inflict final defeat on the Japanese.

On 6 August 1945, a B52 bomber called the 'Enola Gay', captained by Colonel Paul W. Tibbets, carried the first ever atomic bomb to Hiroshima and decimated the city, killing 80,000 people immediately and many more in the years to follow.

Three days later a further atomic bomb was dropped on Nagasaki and the Second World War was over.

When the Americans forced the unconditional surrender, the Japanese Emperor Hirohito was ordered to renounce his heritage to his people; he was not a true God, only a man.

In the five years that Fiszel Lisner had spent in captivity, the whole of Europe was subjected to massive restructure. Not just of buildings and roads, but with what we now call the process of ethnic cleansing. Whole communities were moved and evacuated from specific areas in order to create non-semetic balances in places that were previously inhabited by Jews. By evacuating the Catholics and the Christians and the Lutherans among the communities, Adolf Hitler conversely created areas that were to become wholly Jewish. Lodz, Warsaw, Zdunska-Wola and other large cities in Poland were to be the selected places for massive ghettos. In that country alone, 29 work camps were created. In areas as far south as Croatia and as far north as Stutthof, on the edge of the Baltic Sea, 21 death camps were erected to satisfy the expedient whim of the Nazi pariah.

Within the memories of those who can still remember, names such as Dachau, Auschwitz, Belsen, Buchenwald, Treblinka, Ravensbruck, Mathausen and Jasenovac will remain forever in the minds of the Jews who now inhabit Israel and other countries spread across the face of the globe. These names are alien to the youngsters of the new generation, but they must never be forgotten.

Fiszel never knew that in the city that was closest to his home, shortly after his abduction in 1940, a barbed wire fence was erected around the Lodz ghetto that would restrict 164,000 Jews, including the members of his family, from all contact with the outside world. At first the Germans considered sending them all to the largest ghetto ever created, in a place called Lubinland, southern Poland. But the numbers were too great. Then astonishingly, they considered a mass transport to Madagascar, an island to the east of Mozambique.

Can that idea have been born in the minds of those who could be considered in any way to be sane?

By the end of the year the Germans had run out of ideas, and devoid of these, they left people within the ghetto to starve. Thousands died, most from starvation and depravation, many from indiscriminate raids on their property and person. Not satisfied with the now intolerable conditions they had created, the Nazis then decided to increase the population of the already overcrowded ghetto by transferring a further 20,000 people from Berlin, Prague and Luxembourg. Most of these were cripples, the old and the infirm.

It is thought that many died trying to summon sufficient strength to board the trains, or died before completing the journey, locked as they were inside airless cattle wagons.

Among the final figure of 6,000,000 who perished were many who were deported out of the ghetto for minor transgressions or age or uselessness, to places unknown, never to be heard of again.

Then, the fortunes of war gave the unimaginative controllers of the Lodz ghetto an idea that was designed to increase the war effort. Just like the war camps. Unpaid labour!

By 1942 the Germans had turned the Ghetto into a vast slave labour camp, with the people inside being forced to work for starvation rations making war requisites such as uniforms, shoes and boots, serving whatever were the needs of the army. By 1943, over 127 factories had been set up, employing 80,000 Jews. By this time only 89,000 of the original 184,000 still remained alive. Every human being who could walk, over the age of eight, was put to work from seven each morning until five at night, with just an hour break in order to devour a cup of insipid soup and a mandatory ration of 250 grams of bread each day. The sick and dying, the old and the young, the frail and the immobile received nothing.

I have spoken previously of how the mass deportation from the ghetto was resisted by the elders, but not how one, Hans Biebow, a business administration graduate, was sent by Berlin to persuade the Jews to accept that they were being moved to a better place. This following a secret decision by the hierarchy to exterminate the entire population of the ghetto. Many of the residents were naturally sceptical, but after the graduate had convinced them, most gave way and accepted the order that was to take them to their death.

On 1 June 1941, there were 76,701 Jews still alive at Lodz. By September, over 60,000 had been sent to the gas chambers. In all 164,000 had died during the life of the ghetto. You will recall that Charmel and Bella, Fiszel's cousins, were among the 870 survivors who hid in secret cellars after the final transport, to be freed by the advancing Russians on 19 January.

The story of the Lodz ghetto can be repeated many times. Did the Germans really think they would be able to hide the atrocities? Did they think that the mass graves and the open ditches full of decomposed skin and bone would not be discovered?

I ask again. How did Fiszel Lisner survive five years of this relentless torture? What guiding force protected him, so that he is alive today, 48 years on, to tell us of his experiences? To confirm to the doubters, the non-believers that, yes, it really did happen? 6,000,000! 6,000,000! 80 Yankee Stadiums full of cheering fans. 150 Old Traffords. Half the population of London. All the population of New Delhi. Half of Australia!

The comparisons are innumerable. I mention them in order to create a vision. A vision that must never be seen again.

In the minds of those Jews who can remember it all, but were not a part of it, those who today are in their early-sixties and mid-fifties still experience feelings of guilt and frustration.

How nearly all of them would have wanted to be there, fighting alongside the Allies, freeing their brothers. In the minds of the new generations who have grown up since those dark days is, what? Many who I have spoken to are virtually unaware of these events. Many are aware but choose to ignore them. Most are ignorant of the names, the powers, the circumstances, the times of differing morality, and the demands of nation upon nation that may have been responsible for the twentieth century Holocaust.

Whether you are of Jewish faith or not, whether you are of white skin, brown or yellow, black or red, is not relevant.

What is most important about the life of Fiszel Lisner during the years 1939 to 1945, and many similar to him, although I doubt whether there are many who suffered it all for such a sustained period and lived to tell the tale, is that we learn to forgive but do not forget.

Alf & Hanah Rogers with the soldier brother who arranged
Fiszel's escape to Belgium, 1945.

EsteraLaja - Fiszel's mother at 12, 1916.

Some of Estera-Laja's family, all of whom were murdered
by the Nazis by 1942.

Uncle Charlie (2nd from right, back row), aunty Sylvia (white blouse),
friends and other family members, late summer, Spa, Belgium, 1945.

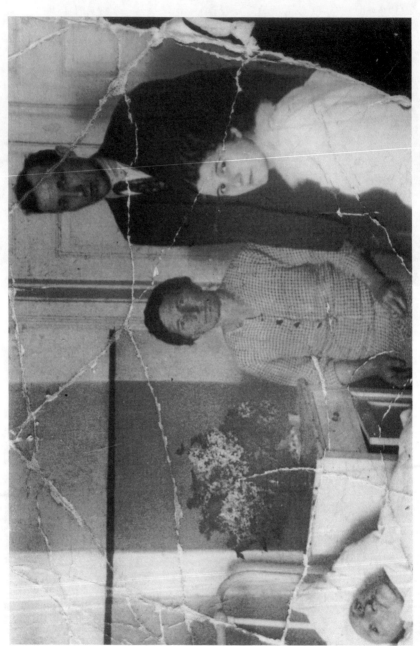

Estera-Laja on her deathbed, November 1939. A neighbour, a nurse and Luzer.

Fiszel in Brussels with son of distant relative who gave him shelter, 1946.

No style - Fiszel in a refugee's hand-out of Italian army uniform (front end right). Enjoying with friends and colleagues, Frankfurt-on-Main, 1946.

Just 2 days before the call came
from Charlie to return to
Bergen-Belsen,
Thursday 12 September 1946.

Friends again-visiting Bella and
Charmel in Israel, 1958.

Henya, Neustadt Holstein, 17 April,
1946.

Chaim Urbach (centre) with
2 brothers, America, 1959.
The same Chaim Urbach who
sponged Fiszel's face and body
while he was "hanged" at the first
Polish work camp, 1940.

Myer, Henya and Fiszel,
Frankfurt-on-Main, 1946.

Healthier now, Fiszel says
farewell, 15 September, 1946.

Saying goodbye to Bendet Lenkowicz,
Bergen-Belsen, September, 1946.

Room-mates at Frankfurt-on-Main.
Fiszel and Myer standing, 1946.

27 May 1946. After 1 year of "BINGING",
ready for England, farewell to
Bergen-Belsen.

PART TWO

CHAPTER 1

ENGLAND 1946-1948

It has been three weeks since I finished Part I. The inspiration to continue has deserted me, partly because I am too distressed, partly because I am suffering from a feeling of anticlimax, but mainly because reviving these memories had caused Fiszel to enter into a pit of depression by day and into sleepless nights accompanied by horrific nightmares.

We have met several times, and we have talked, but it has become somehow impossible to turn on the tape recorder and continue. A period of calm without the pressures of painful recollection is needed.

Fiszel feels ready again to continue.

Perhaps I should begin the second part of his story with a quote from Virgil: a step forwards is to strive for the forbidden.

"Fiszel," I began with my first question. "Tell me more about the clerk who got your birth date wrong on your papers. I am intrigued as to how you came to be born on the 23rd, as against the 2nd, and in the 11th, as against the 1st month. I can understand that the number of your house was 28, and I can see the clerk in my mind's eye writing this down in the year of your birth column instead of the column that asks for your former residence. That sort of thing happens even today."

I could see his mind return to the day he first arrived in the transit camp. It was not pain on his face, more as if he was struggling to see the crowded hall, the line of clerks sitting at their desks, the austere surroundings. The noise. Pandemonium. Refugees, Jewish, noted for their vociferous exclamations and gesticulations, stronger now after weeks of life-returning sustenance, even after the thoughtful British Army officers had tried desperately to moderate their intake and bring them slowly back to normality.

Haltingly, he began his recollection.

"I was in a line of people. They were all talking at once. Two were virtually leaning on my back in their impatience to get to the clerk. He was young and he didn't appear to know much German, and certainly no Yiddish. He asked me questions in English and I made attempts to reply in broken German. Zwei, two, I said, meaning the day of my birth. I repeated it, zwei und ein, two plus one, meaning the day of the month, January. He must have understood me to mean two, plus two and one. 23. I think I must then have repeated the month twice, eins, eins. One, one. Hence, 11. How he came to put down vier und zwanzig, 24, as acht und zwanzig, 28, I have no idea, except that I must have thought he had already put down the full date of birth and was now asking for my home address. You may not believe this, and possibly the readers of this book may not understand but I had endured so much during those five years that I not only did not look at what he was writing down, but I could not have even argued with him about my date of birth, my head was so 'fermished' (mixed up). Do you think the readers will understand, when I tell you that I could not remember it? The only things I knew for certain were my home address, my name, incredibly my uncle Charlie's address in England, and my ever-continuing hunger. Do you know that I had put on nearly three stone in weight since my release? But my mind was in turmoil and I really didn't know what day of the week it was! Can anyone comprehend this? Do you think, Guy, that there is anyone who wasn't there who can truly know what I am talking about?"

I turned the tape off again. I waited for the emotional moment to decline. He was in a sort of rage, and it was Mary told me not to worry about it. He has always been given to emotional outbursts, more so since he decided to recall these experiences.

The boat bringing Fiszel to a new life was delayed by a vicious sea and as a result the connection with the train at Dover was missed. While uncle Charlie and the people from Shelter waited patiently, Fiszel sat with the others waiting for the next train, wondering whether uncle Charlie would still be at Victoria Station.

That was not the only thing on his mind. Memories of his homeland, the friends he had left behind, the fear of the future, all invaded his consciousness during those lonely moments sitting on the platform. For maybe the first time, the loss of his family brought about the deep sorrow that was missing when he originally found out about them and the barbaric way they had met their end. Feelings, emotions, numbed and crushed during almost his entire teenage life, began returning, as the isolation and loneliness invaded his soul and invoked that detached feeling of hallucination he had experienced once before. With little to do while waiting for the train, he wandered the cold, friendless railway station in a dream. So many questions were going through his mind, and so few answers. It might have been after another hour, or it might have been after another minute, Fiszel is unsure, but his return to reality came when one of the others travelling with him tugged on his arm to advise him that the train was on the platform and they were ready to embark.

Now it was all rush, enthusiasm, and excitement as he and the others boarded their first train in the promised land.

At Victoria, uncle Charlie was becoming impatient. He had been waiting for more than four hours, and so, after a word with the organisers of the charity who were meeting the displaced Jews who were coming to England, he duly left, with a message to notify him if and when his nephew finally arrived. Shortly after he had gone on his way, the train bound for London eased its way out of Dover Station.

On arrival in London, Fiszel, tired and clearly frightened, was informed that he would be spending his first night in a centre that was being used as temporary housing for the arrivals, called Isaac Woolfson House. The shock that no member of his family had waited for him, and that once again he would be in some sort of institution, did nothing for his morale.

Following a restless, sleepless night, on the morning of Tuesday 18 September 1946, he was finally freed from all institutional existence when Alf Rogers picked him up in his battered Ford to start the journey into a new life.

Uncle Charlie and aunty Sylvia were rich. No doubt about that. Their spacious condominium in the heart of London's West End provided luxury, totally alien to their bewildered nephew. Situated in the Edgware Road, before it became what it is today, some 200 yards from Hyde Park Corner, Fiszel's relatives had made a life of comfort for themselves with sheer business ability and hard work. It was only after a couple of hours in their presence that Fiszel learned that they had arrived in England in 1920, poor but in love and determined to make a success in their chosen country. At first uncle Charlie had worked as a tailor and cutter in one of the sweat shops of the East End, but he was soon to discover that he would never be able to give to his beloved Sylvia what she craved by working all the hours God created for a few measly shillings. It was after the birth of their first child, a daughter Jenny, that Charlie set up a small factory close to where he had worked previously, to make garments for some of the more prestigious houses with showrooms in places like Bond Street and Great Portland Street. The land of opportunity offered much, and he prospered until he, too, was able to open his own wholesale showrooms along with another Jewish refugee who shared in his dreams of wealth. Clearly uncle Charlie had seen that as a manufacturer and wholesaler, with his own design label, the days of long arduous concentration at the cutting table on the over-locker could all be behind him. The firm of Glicksman and Schneider was open!

Sylvia bore Charlie two further children, daughters Hannah and Betty, and with the proceeds of his successful business they purchased two blocks of flats in South Woodford, Essex, each containing 16 apartments. It was in this environment, so vastly different from his early days of freedom in Zdunska-Wola, that Fiszel found himself sharing in tears and laughter as he sat drinking numerous cups of coffee in those opulent surroundings, recalling the days he had spent with Estera-Laja, Luzer and his sisters and brother. When it came to questions about the five horrendous years of slavery, he feigned tiredness and took himself off to the most luxurious bedroom he had ever slept in. Uncle Charlie knew. Knew that to question the boy was not wise, and as a result, never again asked him about the camps and the marches, and his former existence.

Strangely, at the time, although the British had been well informed about the camps, the death marches, the mass graves, the starvation and the overall treacherous inhumanity of the Nazis, there were still some hostile factions expounding their Fascist sympathies. None more than the infamous Sir Oswald Moseley, a duly elected member of the House of Parliament, kicked out by the Government for his sympathetic attitudes to Hitler. It was because of this continuing insecurity and fear that something akin to what had taken place in Europe could happen here in England, that the resident Jews of this country frequently denied their heritage. Uncle Charlie advised Fiszel that when he was out and about, he should always tell inquisitors that he was from Sweden or Norway, or some such neutral country unassociated with Judaism. He also informed Fiszel that the laws of the land prevented him from obtaining employment in this country for a period of six months following entry, and that the boy should fill his time by attending day school in order to learn the language and history of this country.

For the first month, Fiszel spent the time as a tourist. He visited his cousin Jenny and her husband, also married to an Alf, who lived in Rhyl, and the homes of Hannah and Betty, both of whom were married with children. A family life was beginning to evolve, and Fiszel found the warmth and love that was being given to him both satisfying and comforting. He met again Alf Roger's brother who had visited him in Germany and had been so instrumental in confirming his identity to uncle Charlie and arranging for him to be smuggled across the Belgian border.

The holiday over, uncle Charlie registered the boy in a language school on the Charing Cross Road and Fiszel began his first independent pursuit. It was there that he met a boy of similar age called Leon Mendez. Leon had been in this country about a year longer than Fiszel and had already learned many of the ropes. He began taking Fiszel out to the popular dance halls of the day, the Lyceum, the Palace, the Tottenham Royal, the Charing Cross Astoria, and the Regency Rooms. It was at one of these dances that Fiszel was to rediscover a sexual relationship when he met a girl called Maureen, who was immediately attracted to the dark handsome boy, particularly when he took her in his arms and guided her around the ballroom floor, twisting and turning to the waltz, one of the dances that Leon had taught him when they should have been studying the English language! With his uncle's advice in mind, he told her that he was over here from Sweden, on assignment for his wealthy father. He took her home. She lived alone, but her landlady restricted visiting by the opposite sex. That was to be no obstacle to their intentions, and it was with the excuse that the hotel at which he was staying (one of the best in London at the time, the Dorchester), would be closed and that it was too late to return, that she allowed him to stay the night.

He remembers that girl particularly, for she was the first in a period of promiscuousness in his life, whereby he spent his entire time visiting dance halls, attempting to persuade, and on many occasions succeeding, the prettiest of young ladies to his bed.

It was towards the end of this wild period of his life, at the Astoria Charing Cross Road, during a favourite quickstep and with his command of the English language little improved from the day he arrived, that he first met his wife to be, Yetta. He spoke to her in Yiddish and faltering English. She spoke to him in English and faltering Yiddish. It was also at the end of this period that he was granted his permit to start work. Naturally, he expected uncle Charlie to offer him a job in his organisation, but Charlie refused, on the basis that he disapproved of relatives working under him. Fiszel remembers aunty Sylvia's words when he discussed this situation with her.

"Fiszel, tell me, do you love your uncle?"

"Of course I do, aunty. He has become everything to me. He has paid for the schooling, given me pocket money, allowed me to live here in your home, and I owe him a lot for all that he has done. If he let me work for him, I could pay him back something."

"Your uncle does not need to be paid back," she replied. "What he wants is your continuing respect and love, and he feels that if you work for him he will lose this. How can he shout at you when you do something wrong? Soon, you would learn to resent him and this he doesn't want. Listen to the words of the wise!"

Headstrong and resentful, Fiszel left their home to take up residence in the flat of his friend Leon, who lived with his aunt and uncle and who ran a shop in Cleveland Street, above which they lived in moderate comfort. Leon's parents had been murdered by the Nazis. Fiszel began dating Yetta seriously. Her parents immediately liked the boy, and were particularly impressed by his relatives, who were, naturally, respected among the community even though their paths had not crossed. Having wealthy relatives who resided in London's West End would prove no obstacle to the future plans of their daughter and her beau. It was then that Fiszel fell ill with what he believes to have been a recurrence of the typhus he had caught while in Theresienstadt. Aunty Sylvia responded to a call from Leon, and quickly returned her ailing nephew to her apartment where the finest doctor was called and Fiszel successfully treated.

Following his recovery, during which Yetta visited the Edgware Road apartment, Fiszel still refused to carry on living with his aunt and uncle. The rift between Charlie and his nephew had not been healed, and so, kindly as he always was, Charlie offered Fiszel one of his flats in the South Woodford block. It was then that Fiszel started his first job, as a machinist and stock-cutter in one of the notorious East End sweat shops.

On recollection, Fiszel thinks that the boss was induced to take him on by Charlie, particularly if the man wished to continue making up garments for Glicksman and Schneider!

Fiszel and Yetta continued their friendship, for that was all it was. The morality and respect for his future wife entered into his thinking again, as it had done so disastrously with Henya, and there was nothing more than light petting between the girl and Fiszel, although he remembers that this was not entirely his idea. Yetta refused heavy petting, and any idea of fulfilling their love for each other before the wedding was tantamount to an early divorce.

With two pounds a week coming into his home, and no rent to pay, Fiszel decided to ask Yetta to marry him.

I asked him whether he truly loved her, a poignant question.

"What I needed more than anything at that time was stability and security. Basically, I wanted a family again. My own family. On reflection, and I know that it is a very bad thing to say, I don't now think that we were in love in the true sense of the word. There was nothing thrilling about our relationship. No excitement. No pain in the gut, which I think should always be there when two people fall truly in love. Although the marriage was not arranged, as was the done thing back in my days in Poland, it was sort of accepted by our families that we would marry. It seemed the right thing to do. That is, accepted by everyone except my aunty Sylvia!

Two weeks before the wedding, she and I sat in her living room and she advised me that it was not too late to call it off. She was a very wise lady and saw things that no-one else could, not even Charlie. She told me that Yetta was strange, and that there was something wrong with the girl. I knew that Yetta was a bit highly strung and a bit difficult to get on with at times, but I argued and, of course, I knew best. I know my children will condemn me for saying this, but I think that I should have listened to Sylvia."

On Sunday 11 July 1948, following a five month engagement, and contrary to the wishes of his aunt, Fiszel started his own family when he and Yetta were married at the Jubilee Street Synagogue in Stepney, East London. More than 200 people turned out in splendid tuxedo and ball gown to celebrate the first happiness of the lonely boy who had arrived in this country from the devastation of the Second World War.

Against walls lined with buffet tables enladened with black market sides of smoked salmon, gefilte fish, herrings, smoked meats and salads, and to the resounding rhythm of the 'Hava Nagilah' played at lightning speed by a six-piece orchestra, the guests accompanied the happy couple around the dance floor, arms linked in joyous tribute, unaware that the bride and groom were setting out on a path toward tragedy and sorrow that would begin with its roots cemented in a lamentably discordant honeymoon.

CHAPTER 2

VARIATION OF DEPRIVATION 1948-1963

The Cambridge dictionary describes deprivation as the act of depriving; state of being deprived; want; bereavement.

It also describes deprivation as the deposition of a clergyman. There is of course no logic in deprivation, and as the dictionary fails to mention, degree!

To be deprived of love can, and almost always will, affect the recipient of this emotional chasm adversely. The loss of family, freedom, of liberties, and many other aesthetic deprivations, will have an equally debilitating effect. But these often do not detract from the material quality of life. The emotional strains produced by the absence of these normalities within a human being's life can be traumatic, and in the case of Fiszel Lisner they surely must have been so.

At the time of his marriage, however, he had no doubt endured these traumas, but other than the time when his so-called friends left Theresienstadt with his booty, he had not been subjected to one of the remaining and most humiliating deprivations of all. The one that affects many of us at some time or other. The one that affects the vast majority of the world's populace; that of poverty perpetuated by financial loss.

Who is it that ordains that some among us should be wealthy and others, the masses, spend our existence struggling for those comforts that mean usually a happy and relaxed existence? Who is it that points the finger and chooses the selected few?

Among the many peoples of this Earth are the believers. The ones with faith who universally trust in a fair and honest God. Whether their God is in the *Illiad, The Talmud, The New Testament or The Koran,* their faith cannot be questioned, as it often provides the sanctity they seek. Without faith, we may ask, where are we?

Why is it then that there is so much suffering? Why so much disproportionate distribution of good and evil? Why what seems to be such uneven distribution of wealth?

A spiritualist friend of mine once explained that we are all here on Earth to pass examinations, and when we have reached such levels of goodness following innumerous reincarnations, we would finally pass into Utopia, the true world of God. Heaven! That seems awfully contrived to me. Why doesn't her God make us all good all the time and then we can all live in Utopia? Maybe my reasoning is too pragmatic for the Spiritualists!

Another philosophical man who I knew, in fact a cousin who has just passed away from cancer, once told me that there was only a Heaven, no Hell, as this world in which we dwell was the Hell! A very cynical view. He saw his only obligation as being one to leave a better world, on a purely private level, for his own children.

Who is to say that that is not our obligation? Which of the believers has got it right? All we really know for sure is that we live, we eat, we drink, we procreate, and we die. The rest is conjecture, for above all there seems to be little reason for our lives, which returns me to the question of why should some suffer so much more than others? Why then does Fiszel Lisner have so little 'nachus' in his life, when all of us, even the materially wealthy, have to put up with some adversity. Why should one man be selected to endure so much more than any other?

In the annals of time, in the history of mankind, and within the research of many events that have occurred throughout the ages, I have never encountered the finger of deprivation to be pointed at one man so successfully as the one that aimed at Fiszel Lisner. Some may argue for the disabled who deserve unlimited sympathy, or the starvation of the African tribes, the children in the Romanian institutions, and many, many other instances of injustice and suffering. I could go on forever listing these, but for one man to have such a prolonged and sustained history of monumental misfortune is beyond my comprehension.

May I indulge you in the first of these instances of which I write? The aesthetic, physical and mental forces of evil which Fiszel had endured were, to all intents and purposes, behind him. Or should have been, if there was to be any justice. It really only left the material. Perhaps the eye of the decider would shine its laser-like beam with a proportionate degree of sympathy on him in this area, seeing as how he had suffered all these other deprivations.

Fiszel was engaged to Yetta, and earning his two pounds per week at the sweat shop, when one of his distant relatives, Harry Hodis, took him for a night out at Clapton Greyhound races.

"What do I want to see a load of hounds running round chasing a stuffed 'shmutter' for?", he asked in Yiddish.

"Come with me, you might enjoy it. It's a good night out", his second cousin argued, forced to reply in the same tongue.

"Okay, I come to keep you company."

It was fortunate that the man spoke Yiddish, for at this time, even after attending language school, and being among Englishmen for more than one year, Fiszel's brain could still not understand our tongue.

It was Bank Holiday Monday. The morning meeting had attracted a big crowd from Hackney and Stamford Hill and Clapton itself, districts inhabited by many Jewish people who are known to enjoy the art of gambling, just a little! Watching the six dogs being walked round before the first race, Fiszel asked his compatriot what he had to do.

"You look at the programme. You pick out two dogs by their numbers, and you go to the office up there, these small windows, and ask for a reverse forecast."

"What's a reverse forecast?"

"What's a reverse forecast? Don't they have greyhound racing in Poland? It means you pick out two dogs who have to finish in first and second place. Then you give the lady some money, in units of one penny, and you wait and watch, and if your two numbers finish in either order you win."

"What if one wins and one comes in third?"

"You lose!"

"Seems hard to pick one dog to finish first let alone two to finish together."

"Here, look at your programme. Pick two numbers."

"I can't even read the names."

"Names, shnames. Just pick two numbers. I go with you the first time and show you how to bet."

"Here, these two."

"Oy vay! You got no chance. One is third favourite and the other hasn't got in the frame for a month. They lowered him down to A10."

"What's A10?"

"Every dog runs in a class of race. If he don't win A1, they put him A2 and so on. He comes down the scale until he finds similar runners who run at about the same speed."

"How do they know this. Does the dog say to another one, how fast are you going to run today?"

"Schlemiel! The racing manager gives each dog a trial and then he gets an idea how fast the animal can run, and so he puts him in with similar dogs. You want to change your mind about the numbers you picked?"

"No, I come with you, I put a shilling on the reverse forecast. How much is that going to cost me?"

"The last of the big 'schpielers' you are! A whole two shillings you bet. I usually bet ten bob, or sometimes a knicker. Cost me a pound or two a bet."

"Look, first time I bet two bob, after that we see."

"You'll be chasing your losses with these selections."

Fiszel held his tickets tightly in his hand, watching the 31-second race. His selections finished first and second!

"Hey, I won! How much I get?"

"You wait until the light shows on that board over there. The first amount is for the winner. The second light shows how much you get if you bet the second dog, and the third light over there shows how much you get for having the first and second. It'll be a good amount. Both weren't fancied in the betting."

"How do you know which dogs are fancied?"

"You watch the bookmakers over there. They write the prices they are laying for each dog. The other way is to watch the big lit up board, the one with the flashing lights. They show you the number of bets on each dog and the number of units on each forecast."

"The lights are up. That first one says nine shillings, and that one says four and sixpence. Hey, the one for the forecast says one pound and ninepence. Is that what I win?"

"I should be so lucky! You win almost a month's wages on your first bet! It must be beginner's luck! Now I tell you something. Because you are having your first bet, I thought I might have a side bet the same as yours. I bet a couple of pounds. Here, you can have ten pounds of my winnings to bet on the rest of the races. Who'd believe I won a fortune following a 'schmo' like you."

At the end of the six-race meeting, Fiszel had selected five winning forecasts, ending with a profit of £74.11s 6d! Nine months of slogging at the cutting bench in one enjoyable morning!

On the Thursday following his first visit he returned with Harry and this time had an almost equal degree of success. He bet four winning forecasts, laid out as much as ten shillings in each race and ended up £68.13s 6d to the good. Unaccompanied on his third visit, but certain that the good Lord above was smiling on him, providing money for the forthcoming wedding and an expensive honeymoon, he confidently approached the forecast window and began to place his bets again.

At the end of the meeting he had lost in every race and was £137.00 down. Every penny he had so fortuitously collected, plus some of his own money, had been lost, and he was, naturally, once again deprived.

Some would say that it was self-deprivation. The incident is a futile exercise in demonstrating his continued misfortune, but who above ordained his losses? What eternal plan would have been ruined if he were allowed to go on winning and accumulating a little wealth? More adversity was to follow.

The guests had all but left, save for the bride and groom and Yetta's parents. They remained behind for the honoured obligation of paying the 'Kosher' caterer in cash so that he could settle with his staff and suppliers, and of course retain the profits. That would enable him to return to his family with his hard-earned spoils, probably, being Jewish, with the intention of stopping off on the way home to have a quick go on a roulette table at the local casino, or to attend a late night illegal card session at one of the notorious upstairs snooker halls that were dotted around the East End at that time.

The problem was, however, that after paying the deposit on the planned honeymoon for his daughter and her new husband, old man Hyman Singler, Yetta's father, did not have the necessary funds required to meet the caterer's bill. How he managed to carry off the whole evening knowing that at the end of it there would be this problem was a tribute to his cavalier style.

It may seem amusing, but it was not a scene of merriment that ensued, for the caterer was a hard man and wanted his money. By tradition it was the honourable way that the father of the bride paid for his daughter's finest day. The man ranted and raved, and threatened in no uncertain terms, but to no avail. Even the promise of legal action would not solve his problem of paying the staff who were waiting for their wages in the kitchens, unaware of the drama that was taking place outside in the hall.

Uncle Charlie had already gone home, and in any case he had paid for the liquor and had presented Fiszel with a handsome cheque to 'get the happy couple on their way' as had virtually all the other guests.

This was another tradition. Jews, like Greeks, do not buy presents; they give cheques and cash in envelopes!

As Yetta sat on Fiszel's lap, sobbing, her parents argued and tried desperately to negotiate themselves out of the embarrassing situation, with promises of payment in one month, or by spreading the amount over four payments, even suggesting that the caterer add a small amount for interest. All to no avail. Eventually the wedding presents became the subject of the caterer's vociferous demands.

"Give me the presents, and then you can pay back the bride and groom in any way you want. I just hope that there is enough cash among the cheques to pay the staff."

The caterer was adamant. Fiszel handed him the envelopes. How little dignity there was at that moment as the man, now joined by his head waiter, began to rip the envelopes open and accumulate their contents. The account for the food, the band and the hall hire came to £415.00. In the envelopes was a total amount of £355.00. A shortfall of £65.00. Fiszel had no choice but to make his excuses so that he could visit the cloakroom where he had placed a suit of day clothes, ready to start his honeymoon. In the pocket was almost all his savings, about £80.00. He withdrew the balance needed and paid the difference out of his own pocket. After paying for a taxi he had a total of £10.00 remaining to take his bride on honeymoon, when they arrived back at his apartment in Woodford for their first night together. The mood was hardly conducive to a romantic, champagne-induced night of sexual passion! Still in tears, Yetta went to their bed and slept, while Fiszel waited impatiently for the morning so that he could ring uncle Charlie to ask him for a loan. At dawn's early light he telephoned his uncle, who listened with anger and alarm to Fiszel's account of the events of the night before. It was then that Charlie told Fiszel that he had forgotten to give him an envelope that had arrived from his brother-in-law who lived in Texas and which contained one hundred dollars, which Charlie would naturally change into Sterling in order to allow his nephew to take his bride to her honeymoon.

The first night spent in Cliftonville, in Kent, at a moderately inexpensive boarding house was a disaster and was to set the pattern of disillusionment and sexual frustration for the remainder of their married life. Fiszel, now an experienced lover, was eager to make love to his bride, but she was totally unable to respond. The evening ended with Fiszel walking along the sea front, lonely and confused by his wife's resistance to his physical needs. They spent the next day in awkward togetherness, visiting the sights, lunching at a local fish restaurant, and apprehensively awaiting the night. Still unable to consummate their marriage, Yetta and Fiszel argued, and once again she lay tearfully in her lonely bed, while Fiszel paced the deserted promenade. By morning Fiszel had rejoined his wife, weariness and isolation his motivation. He tried to comfort her. He spoke quietly and reassuringly to her. He held her close and allowed her to feel the warmth of his body and the needs of his being. On the third night, Yetta lay beneath him, unresponsive, reluctantly yielding to the physical demands upon her person.

For that is how she saw the act of physical union.

I was forced to ask Fiszel a most personal question. I apologised for the necessity.

"Was Yetta a virgin?" I tentatively enquired.

"To my surprise, she was not?" he answered slowly.

When an author writes someone's biography, he will quickly ascertain when something is wrong, or when the subject is struggling for truth, or for recollection. The author will know when to resist the urge to ask leading questions, or to pursue his subject with unrestrained diligence. On this occasion I knew instinctively that something was wrong, very wrong. Okay, Jewish girls may be no different from any others. She may value her virginity with the same intensity of any other woman of any other denomination. She may also yield to the needs of her body, while casting off the warnings of her parents and the shame that society imposes upon her.

Not Yetta Singler!

She had repeatedly denied Fiszel any flexibility in their physical relationship during courtship. She had not shown any inclination toward the physical; the morality of those times generally meant that respectable girls of eastern European heritage did not make love before they were married. I hope that Yetta's persona, style and character, nervous, intent, highly strung, will allow the reader to agree with my assessment of her at that time.

How then was she not 'intact' when Fiszel finally made love to her?

I watched his face harden and his eyes lower as I sat and pursued the question further. I waited. The atmosphere in the room clouded and thickened.

Finally, he told me of the problem.

"I never found out until fairly recently, but this is a frank account of my life and I do not think that I should keep this secret from you or the readers."

"If it is anything bad, Fiszel, you must trust me to write it with sympathy. Anything that you did, or have done since your release from the camps can be excused, I promise you. I do not think that anyone reading your story will condemn you for anything that you may have done, short of murder."

He smiled wryly.

"It is not anything that *I* did. 40 years after that honeymoon, I found out why she was so, how do you say it, so, so."

"Reticent?"

"Yes, reticent. You see, my Yetta had been sexually abused by her father since she was 12 years old. Even during our courtship and engagement!"

I sat staring with disbelief.

"Did she never tell?" I enquired tentatively.

"I learned this only three years ago. Perhaps if she had told me, I might have had more sympathy for her. Might have understood more about why she found the physical side of our marriage so repulsive. Not that we didn't have our moments. There were times when we were happy, or maybe when things seemed to be going particularly well, that she responded, and that side of things was a little more fulfilling, but in the main it got down to me taking and her giving, reluctantly, and suffering the consequences. In those days girls weren't like they are today! They were taught by their mums that sex was a chore and a duty It's difficult to say what might have been if I had known."

"I don't want to pre-empt 1988 when you found this all out, so I won't push you into telling me how you came to discover this dark secret," I countered.

"It's okay, no problem. I was talking to the girls, and to Larry (Fiszel's son), and they told me that Yetta was always inquiring as to whether daddy had touched them and things like that. So I asked why she asked them that. It was something that quite shocked me. I've read about such things, but for me to be like that is unbelievable. How could she have even thought such a thing. Larry told me that he asked Yetta why she was always asking them, and it was then that she told him. The children decided to keep it a secret until just a few years ago, like I told you."

Life is full of absurdities, which strangely enough do not even need to appear plausible since they are true!

Fiszel and Yetta returned from honeymoon, the pattern of their lives set by what happened in Margate, and life continued with him still working at the machine and on the cutting table, until August, one month after the wedding, when Yetta announced she was pregnant. Fiszel received a one pound per week raise in salary, and on 1 May 1949 their first child, a girl they named after Estera-Laja, Estelle, was born in a hospital in Mile End. It was a difficult birth, but Yetta recovered quickly and returned home to the elated Fiszel. Estelle filled their lives. Fiszel doted on her while Yetta called upon the help of her mother to nurse and tend the new born child. Shortly after this, Yetta fell pregnant again, and a son, Larry (named after Luzer), was born to them on 24 August 1950.

Incredibly, Fiszel still chose to speak Yiddish, and sometimes Polish, but only occasionally his new tongue, which he was still finding difficult to learn. Relations with Yetta were strained further by this inability to learn English.

When the third child, Maralyn, was born, coincidentally on exactly the same day as Larry, one year later, Fiszel, prompted by his wife and first daughter, decided to make the effort to learn our language properly.

It is all credit to him that he fired his brain into action with dogged determination, and strangely, within just a few months, everything fell into place. He was now reading and writing and becoming more anglicized.

The flat became clearly overcrowded, with two adults and three children sleeping in one room, and well-appointed as the premises were, it was clear that a larger place was needed. Fiszel applied to the council and was given a two-bedroomed house, still in the Woodford area, which was seemingly fortuitous, as his boss died at that time and the factory was closed down by his widow.

Fiszel was out of work for six months during which time he signed on, which provided him with some income and a continuance of health service stamps. Eventually, forced by ever increasing poverty, he went to see his uncle Charlie who listened and suggested that he provide the money for Fiszel to open a business. Fiszel, elated, told his gambling friend, Harry, who suggested that, as his wife was a first class cook, they should open a cafe in partnership. Charlie agreed, and after making Harry and Fiszel sign a loan agreement with his solicitors in attendance, he advanced them £800.00.

'The Continental Rest' opened its doors to the public in the autumn of 1951 and was an immediate success. Trading on each and every day of the week, they offered cups of tea for a penny ha'penny and cooked meals for as little as two and sixpence or three shillings.

It was when the cafe had been open for about eight months that Fiszel discovered some extraordinary statistics. It seemed that whenever Harry was on duty in the early hours, before Fiszel arrived, the takings were always more than Fiszel had rung up when the rotas were reversed. Fiszel could not understand this. He worked as hard. He always opened the premises on time. In order that Harry and his wife should not think that he was fiddling the till, he began putting in his own money. This system continued until Fiszel began feeling the pinch. One day he asked Leon to visit the cafe when Harry had the early morning shift and to watch what his partner did that resulted in the increased takings. Leon enjoyed his stint as private detective and reported to Fiszel that Harry was emptying the public telephone pay box and putting the takings into the till.

Fiszel took his partner to task and Charlie called in the accountants. They remonstrated with the two businessmen and advised them that the reason for the cafe being so busy was because they were selling their product for less than the items cost, and their best plan, in view also of the mistrust between them, was to sell.

In 1952, 'The Continental Rest' was sold, surprisingly at a profit, which allowed them to pay Charlie back and retain some savings. Fiszel then applied to the Raeback Company for a job and was taken on as a machinist until 1953 when two events gave him the opportunity to start another business, more this time in his normal line of work and experience.

The German Government, under Konrad Adeneur, agreed to make reparation payments to those Jews who had suffered such adversity under Nazi rule as to impair their current existence. The amount would be determined by the degree of inability, and for any underpayment made for work carried out on construction sites. The autobahn that Fiszel had worked on was a high profile project and he was invited to attend a medical to determine his reward. He had had many twinges and suffered intermittent pain during and ever since his time in the camps and on the marches. It was then that he was told that permanent damage had been done to his Latissimus Dorsus, and that he might one day expect to be totally disabled. His fingers too were showing signs of arthritis and his feet were an abomination. Psychologically he still suffered from nightmares and feelings of detachment and heart palpitations. (He has taken Digoxin 125 for as long as he can remember, to control these, but no permanent defect to his heart has been diagnosed. The conclusion is that he suffers from these palpitations as a result of his experiences between 1939 and 1945).

The doctor decreed that Fiszel was 70 per cent disabled. Fiszel refused the prognosis. He knew that level of disability would affect the whole of his working life and he wanted no part of it. Naturally he was frightened that when his employers found out about it they would surely sack him. He also knew that insurance to protect his family would cost so much more. After considerable discussion and argument, the local doctor wrote a 40 per cent disability on his examination report. The next requirement was for this to be verified by a doctor of German descent, appointed by the consulate. The German doctor agreed with the level of disability, naturally and willingly, and for his degree of sufferance and for the underpayment of his labours, Adeneur's Government awarded Fiszel a pension payment of £8.00 per month plus a one-off payment of £600.00. Generous to a fault for all that Fiszel Lisner had been through. Five years of unbelievable suffering measured in a few measly Deutchmarks. Today that would add up to around £25,000.

With these proceeds and the little interest that the money incurred, Fiszel again formed a partnership, this time with two other tailors who he knew, who had also survived the Nazi occupation of Poland, Johnny Gutman and Issy Harper.

Feeling as he still does today about his new country, Fiszel chose the earliest possible occasion to become a citizen of the United Kingdom, the ceremony of this monumental event taking place on 15 April 1955.

It was at this time that Fiszel came into contact with a Polish/American who was over here on holiday. While at a club the two men met by chance and Fiszel discovered that the man, Dave Bauer, knew of the whereabouts of Bendet and his sisters who had emigrated to the States after leaving Sweden. Fiszel immediately contacted another relative who lived in New York and made plans to go alone to the States.

On arrival he immediately fell ill with his troublesome back and spent the duration of his holiday lying on the floor of his relative's lounge and also that of Bendet's in his home in Detroit. At that time he was able to renew his friendship with Bendet's five sisters who had managed to emigrate from their hideaway in Sweden. Just before the time came for him to return home, Myer, of the black market American Zone base at Frankfurt-on-Main fame, visited, and old times were recalled with both sadness and pleasure. It was Myer who told Fiszel that Chaim Ber Urbach, the very one who had saved his life by surreptitiously stealing into the freezing night while he hung by his wrists at the first work camp way back in 1940, was also in New York where he lived with his two brothers. Fiszel found the time to meet again this incredible man and they shared sorrows of the past, and torrents of tears, as each recalled his bitter experiences. It seems that Chaim was always to be a leader, and it was this ablility to be subservient, but never to serve, that enabled him to survive the dreadful holocaust.

Fiszel then returned to England, elated with the meetings that had taken place, steeped as they were in nostalgia and regret, particularly with five sisters who had managed to somehow stay together and make a life for themselves in the other great democracy of the world. He admits to feeling a great sense of remorse that he did not find out about the girls' successful migration before marrying Yetta, because one of the five girls was a particular love from his early days, and the spark of affection was still there when they met again. It was at La Guardia Airport, as he was saying good-bye to Myer, that his old compatriot told him that Henya too had made it out of Europe and was living in America, now married. Fiszel was pleased that he had not learned of this earlier, for there would have been the temptation to visit her and make every effort to renew the love they had felt for each other.

It was therefore little wonder that he returned to this country disillusioned and frustrated.

It was now 1957. The company thrived with the contacts that the formidable uncle Charlie put their way, and not long after they had established their enterprise, the premises in the Minories became too small. The successful company of Trio-Modes Ltd moved to larger premises in Commercial Street.

Everything went well. Fiszel learned to drive and bought himself a

Ford Prefect.

Perhaps the 'shining one' was smiling on him at last! Yetta fell pregnant again, and on 9 May 1958, a third daughter, Suzanne, was born, but not before Yetta had to spend six months in confinement in a local hospital after contracting severe toxaemia. The birth was difficult and Yetta spent much time in recuperation while the children were farmed out to her parent's place in the East End and homes of other relatives. The family became divided, and Fiszel, now deeply engrossed in a thriving business venture, had little opportunity to visit his children. When he did find time to visit Yetta, their meetings were strained and often he left her bedside in disharmonious frustration.

Have you, my readers, realised that, coincidentally, it was 'Beshert'? Yetta had borne Fiszel three daughters and one son. During those dark days of the Second World War, Fiszel had lost three sisters and one brother. In his desperate attempt to form his own loving family he had replaced each of those who had been lost to him on a one for one basis!

What was it that Luigi Pirandello, said about the absurdities of life being plausible for their truth?

When the baby was one year old, with life seemingly going quite well, except for the relationship between Yetta and Fiszel, everything tumbled around him.

Yetta's doctor sent for Fiszel and advised him that the physical side of his relationship with his wife would have to be modified drastically owing to the damage that the birth of the last child had caused, and moreover Yetta was not to fall pregnant again as this might well be fatal for her. Then he was attacked by an Alsatian, which resulted in a heavy fall and a spinal defect that rendered Fiszel totally unsuitable for work. He was rushed into the West

London hospital in agony. For five weeks he lay in traction, unable to move without excruciating pain, unrelieved by pain killers, even when morphine was administered. After failing to cure his condition, the hospital moved Fiszel to the neurological ward of the Dean Street Hospital for an operation. It was then that the ever-increasingly frustrated and highly strung Yetta visited him and demanded that Fiszel buy her a bigger house, while also telling him that during his period of hospitalisation, his two partners had not paid her one penny of his wages.

The nurses had to physically remove Yetta as the argument that resulted reached a vociferous crescendo and was disturbing the other patients. Oblivious to Fiszel's pain and anger with his partners, she blindly demanded that he allowed her to purchase a house she had seen in Redbridge.

Fiszel discharged himself before the planned operation in order to take matters up with Johnny and Issy, who had not visited him once while he lay immobile in either of his hospital beds.

From a telephone beside the sofa upon which he lay, he spoke to the two men who rejected his approach, and so subsequently Fiszel found himself needlessly engaged in legal proceedings.

He was being denied access to the factory and was receiving no pay or return for his investment. With the shares equally divided, he was entitled to one third of the proceeds. Suddenly, to add to his problems, he found himself involved with mortgage applications and additional expense as Yetta had done no more than leave the hospital and immediately place a deposit on the house in Redbridge, clearly in defiance of Fiszel's argument.

Fiszel reluctantly went along with his wife's ill-conceived plan, assured by his solicitors that he had a water-tight case, and that victory would ensue, with beneficial financial gains as the result.

On the steps of the Law Courts, after Fiszel's solicitors had discovered a possible fraudulent sale of his shares, which may have been perpetrated by his partners, the other side agreed to settle. On his lawyer's advice, Fiszel accepted the offer and later was handed a cheque for less than £50.00!

The solicitors had taken almost the entire settlement against their own costs.

Material adversity and depravation were complete. The entire sphere of almost every type of loss had engulfed his life.

There was little left to suffer.

Recovering from this event, his illness, his reluctant move to a new house, his wife's increasing unreasonableness, with four children to support, Fiszel took the family on a holiday to Bournemouth. But they spent only two days away, as Larry went down with a virus and was rushed into a local hospital to seek the courage that must have been in his genes to survive the almost fatal attack. The family returned home, leaving the boy in hospital, and managed only occasional visits, but somehow with sheer strength of character Larry survived and returned home to London none the worse for wear.

It was when Fiszel and the family returned home from this latest disaster that Yetta chose this time to tell her husband that she was beleaguered by debts which she had run-up without his knowledge. Fiszel dealt with the situation, but the matter had driven a further wedge between the now mentally ailing Yetta and her husband. The birth of Suzanne and all that she had endured was beginning to have its affect on her stability. A further heated argument ensued, and Fiszel, for the first time in his life, as he is basically a shy man, lost his temper and, out of control, proceeded to smash up the family home. Wedding photographs, pictures carefully hung on walls, glasses and china were to receive their demise as he uncontrollably suffered a brain seizure, brought about by years of suffering, frustratingly tolerated in order to survive, all of which had never been released. Basically, he just 'cracked-up' and Yetta was to receive the full torrent of his previously withheld emotions.

It is to his credit that he laid not one finger on any member of his family, not even the instigator of his wild act, Yetta. The effect of this outburst, which was to create an impenetrable gap between him and his wife, was to render the poor woman even more reclusive and even less stable.

As in most marriages, they temporarily recovered after the unseemly row and Fiszel quickly returned to normality, but he was now sleeping most nights on a sofa in the lounge.

Fiszel was to once again seek the deserved reward from his labours when he mustered some £300.00 to form another company, this time in league with a female partner whom he had come to know while working in the tailoring trade, affectionately known as the 'schmutter game'.

Immediately, the business side of life again proved to be of some success, but his personal life remained difficult, cold and unrewarding. All that he had sought, a new family, love and affection of close relatives, had turned sour for him.

The nightmares increased and he began feeling depressed and mixed up, as well as continually ill from the pains in his back. Never one to give in, as has been proved on so many occasions in this biography, he actually managed for a while to provide his family with a reasonable existence.

Then, one day, just after he had arrived at the factory, a neighbour called him to advise him that Yetta had tried to take her own life by firstly placing a gas poker in her mouth and then by attempting to jump from their first floor window. Only Larry had saved her, by pulling the poker away from her and following her upstairs and holding on to her skirts while she pulled and tugged, desperately trying to end it all from her position on the window-ledge. The neighbour had sent for an ambulance and she was taken to the Goodmayes hospital. Fiszel raced back to see her but was not allowed access. Her condition was very poor and the specialists were gravely concerned about her mental condition. Yetta's mother was sent for and an au pair engaged to look after the children.

After Yetta had been in the hospital for around six months, Fiszel persuaded the staff to allow him to take her on a planned day-trip with the family to Southend.

It was to be a disaster.

They had travelled only as far as Romford, some four miles away, when Yetta attempted suicide again, this time by swallowing several tablets which she had stolen from the hospital, and then by trying to leap out of the moving car. The police arrived, fortuitously, as they happened to be following and were concerned at the irregular driving pattern when Fiszel tried to reach over to prevent Yetta from leaping out. Yetta was then returned to the hospital to start a downward trend which would ultimately result in a further extended period of frequent hospitalization, but not before further adversity of the most extreme nature was to affect the family.

Estelle had reached 14 and it was the year of Larry's barmitzvah. The year when the male child became a man. The one to carry on the name that had all but vanished some 18 years previously.

Yetta, semi-recovered, was able to attend and share in the proud day. Fiszel was now 39. It was 1963.

CHAPTER 3

THE YEARS 1963-1977

I am writing this chapter in April 1993, although it relates to the Lisner family life during the years 1963-1977.

I mention this only because I needed to verify some dates which were obscure to Fiszel (you will understand why later in this chapter), with his son, Larry. To do this I was to visit him in Heron Ward of a mental institution here in Essex called Runwell Hospital. As one enters the vast expanse of fields and well laid-out gardens, passing the nurses' quarters, one gains the impression that one is entering a military camp. The wards are low, one-storey buildings, lined up side-by-side as in a barracks or even a camp. It reminds me of Fiszel's description of the second work camp that he was sent to. Not that I mean this in a derogatory way, and in no way should my description detract from the excellent work the medics carry out in the hospital. They have drug addicts seeking recovery, depressives and schizophrenics, as well as long term patients who will never recover sufficiently to take their place in the world. There are, to my knowledge, at least two wards that house patients who are regarded as dangers to themselves and to others, but quietly and efficiently the hospital staff deal with all of these to the best of their abilities.

Larry was in one of the temporary patients wards for the sudden onset of depression. He had sought the guidance of his G.P. because of a trauma that had entered his life.

I visited, not only to obtain information, but also to give him a lift and to ask whether he could call on his genes and fight the depression so that his stay might be a short one.

What has all this got to do with the life of Fiszel Lisner?

What indeed you may ask! Larry's admission into Runwell completes a most remarkable cycle, for he is the final member of Fiszel's family to have such mental agonies and difficulties coping with their lives, to either enter, or be advised to do so, one of these institutions. Yetta, later Estelle, Maralyn and Suzanne have all been subjected to this type of medical care at one time or other.

I relate this out of time also because I have spent many weeks searching for the truth. I have not been able to write this chapter until now mainly because I have been asking pertinent and personal questions in my search for the reasons why the members of Fiszel's family have suffered so much during their lives. And yet Fiszel himself has not ever been subjected to such severe mental agonies or breakdowns that necessitated admission to a mental institution. I asked Mary whether she had any ideas on why they had all suffered so badly. I asked Fiszel himself. I asked Larry.

Maralyn is at this time unwell, suffering from post-natal depression, and Suzanne avoids me as she is not entirely in favour of her father telling his story after so many years. Only Larry is really helpful, and from him I am able to gauge some idea of the difficulties that the children experienced during their formative years. But then came the question as to whether his assessment was correct.

Are any children correct in their evaluation of their parents? Don't they all see us as part ogre, part angel? Don't all the parents on this earth have enormous difficulties when the fledgelings seek to flee the nest? No, I am not able to accept Larry's conclusions.

The questions? Did they all suffer because of Yetta's upbringing? Did they all suffer because Yetta was highly strung and unstable? Is it in their genes? Was it their father's upbringing in the strict authoritarian times of eastern Europe and his resultant demands upon them? Or was it that their loving father was unable to demonstrate affection and trust as a result of what happened to him during all those years under Nazi control?

I draw no conclusions. Perhaps, you, my readers, may form your own opinions from what has happened in the years that followed.

Yetta seemed to have recovered sufficiently to take her place in the family life, spurred on by Larry's barmitzvah and by the guilt that she must have felt in missing much of their formative years. Fiszel himself was as involved as could be expected, but the demands of visiting the hospital, visiting the children who were farmed out temporarily, and running the new business were great. When they all returned home from the barmitzvah which was held in a hotel in Margate, owned by a distant relative, Yetta was bright and seemingly normal, but her relationship with her husband had not improved.

By this time, starved of the love that he so desperately sought, Fiszel had started to live a new life. Virtually every night was spent out with friends and relatives. Dancing clubs, casinos and a return to the evening greyhound meetings became the pattern of his social life. It mattered not what time he arrived home, or indeed whether he arrived home at all, as he slept in the lounge, alone, and deprived of family affection.

Where was the fault in all this? Should he have made more effort to encourage Yetta to take him back to her bed? Should he have involved himself more in the day-to-day life of the children?

"I wanted so much and achieved so little. Sex with Yetta was a complete nonentity, and the children fixed their attention to their mother, always suspicious of her stability but always over-compensating with love and affection. It really is understandable. I seemed like a stranger in my own home. When Yetta did speak to me it was about the kids, or money or some 'do' that we had to go to. I tried. I really did. I took them to relatives and picnics and things on the weekends, but it all meant nothing."

Infidelity is an act that society frowns upon, even though statistics show that a high percentage of the population stray the marital line every now and then. Some seriously.

In 1963, the year Profumo showed what a great time could be had with a little subterfuge, and the year when the most popular of American presidents was ruthlessly murdered, Fiszel was faced not only with his personal and emotional difficulties, but with a national sexual explosion. The whole country seemed to be invaded by a new wave of pop music, infidelity, promiscuity and a level of permissiveness not previously imagined. He was youngish, virile, and a man who had less female contact when it mattered most than practically anyone alive.

It was therefore inevitable that he should find comfort in the arms of another. (I find myself excusing his behaviour.)

What started out as a means of escaping a loveless home and an indifferent wife by going out with the boys soon became a web of deceit and lies and excuses, which clearly added to the strains and stresses of his life.

The chicken and the egg!

The woman was 12 years younger than Fiszel, married to an indifferent husband, and seeking to satisfy her needs elsewhere. The time was ripe, the partners vulnerable and acquiescent.

The affair continued throughout the 1960s until Fiszel discovered the woman making love to another at one of their many places of clandestine meetings. An argument ensued which resulted in a fist fight for which Fiszel paid due compensation.

All during this period, the girls Estelle and Maralyn were growing into beautiful young ladies.

It was when Estelle began coming home later than Fiszel himself, that he began to exercise his parental authority. Estelle in particular, when she had reached the age of 17 in 1966, was joining the new wave with dedicated enthusiasm, and arguments took place about the company she was keeping and the hours she was spending away from home. Yetta in turn was not supportive and reasoned with Fiszel that Estelle was young and was just sowing a few wild oats; it was a sign of the times! But Fiszel would have none of it, and he brought to bear upon his eldest daughter the authoritarian attitudes of his own parents.

Two years passed in unquestionable acrimony. Then in 1968, Maralyn suffered a broken romance.

For once, Fiszel was not unhappy with one of his children's choice of partner, when his second eldest girl began courting a wealthy Jewish boy. But it was not to be! This time it was the boy's parents who objected to the relationship. They did not wish for their only son to consider a serious affair with a daughter of a lowly Jewish tailor. Eventually, the threat of excommunication and considerable financial sufferance caused the boy to end his relationship with Maralyn.

It was immediately after this that the first of Fiszel's children entered a mental hospital. Maralyn had suffered a complete nervous breakdown.

Back at the house Estelle was now rowing and arguing with her father to such an extent that she decided to leave home and live with a friend. Fiszel was convinced that she was in with the wrong crowd and that her friends were unsavoury and probably into drugs and crime. His suspicions were later proved correct. But Maralyn was the immediate problem.

In the mental hospital she met another patient called Chas. He too had suffered a breakdown, and the proximity of their existence and their affinity with each other's problems was to cause Maralyn to return home from the hospital and announce her intention of marrying her new found friend.

The boy was not Jewish, and his mental state caused Fiszel to have doubts about Maralyn's wisdom in choosing a partner who was equally as vulnerable as herself and clearly not ready for the responsibilities of marriage. Fiszel therefore strongly objected to the union. The relationship continued against his wishes and in November 1973 Maralyn married her man. Yetta attended the ceremony at a registry office despite Fiszel's clear objections, while he worked at his factory.

Earlier, before the start of the decade, Yetta's mother had died. Estelle had been involved in a car accident and the company dissolved because one of the most important employees, a presser called Morrie, who had also invested some money in the organisation, became too ill to work. The accountants took over the firm with a liquidation order, but once again Fiszel was to try his hand at self-employment, immediately setting up a new factory. In May 1974, Estelle returned home one day to announce that she was to be married. Her suitor was an Italian boy who had been married twice previously and had a son by one of his wives. He was considerably older than Estelle, street-wise, flash, and every girl's dream of the smooth handsome Latin, with dark skin and black curly hair, deep sensual eyes, and a way of speaking that could melt a woman's resolve at 20 paces!

Fiszel hated him on sight, and another argument was to take place, which finally ended with Fiszel disowning his eldest daughter.

From that day on, until she actually had left her husband, she was never to visit when Fiszel was at home, and he would not see or entertain her husband ever again. Yetta went to the wedding, again against her husband's wishes, and Fiszel carried on working in the factory. By this time he was almost a stranger in his own home. His involvement with his wife and children was almost nonexistent and his disillusionment such that all togetherness had been lost as the years of trauma and disagreement continued. Larry was, perhaps, the only child who now communicated at any reasonable level with his father, while Yetta lived in a world of her own, in touch with her children, but completely oblivious to her husband's existence. Fiszel's aims, originating from the deprivation that he had suffered all those years previously, were now in tatters.

As if the lonely loveless life was not enough to contend with, disaster of the most horrendous kind was just around the corner.

In 1977 Estelle's marriage broke down and she left Biero to pick up the threads of an existence, but not before she had attempted suicide on at least three occasions, each time calling for help which arrived at just the right time to save her life. Frequent admissions to two mental institutes took place and her husband added to her pain with constant demands to return and try again, although it was clear that there was no love between the two of them anymore.

On 9 September 1977 Estelle died in a train accident that has to this day remained a mystery to Fiszel and many of the family members.

Her death was deemed to be caused by her own hand and it is recorded that she committed suicide. There are however many unanswered questions. After Fiszel related the details to me I felt the obligation to examine the facts.

If I am to write a true story of my subject's life, then I cannot allow this unsolved mystery to continue without thorough investigation and research.

I telephoned Scotland Yard. I spoke to a telephonist who seemed confused, but eventually suggested that I ring either Hampstead or Paddington Police stations. I rang Hampstead.

"You want records, but I don't think that they keep this sort of information for more than three years". I rang records.

"Records?" After nine minutes of waiting to be answered, "I'll put you through."

"No, we only keep these sort of records for ....Oh, suicide you say? In that case you need to speak to the branch. We are accident records. You know, car accidents etc."

I rang Paddington. Six minutes.

"You have the wrong station sir. We do not deal with things in the Swiss Cottage area. You need Hampstead!"

I rang Hampstead.

"I think that you need C.I.D., but they are all out on an enquiry at the moment. Can I ring you back? I'll ask one of them to call you. They should be back in about an hour."

Two hours passed by. Three. I called again!

"I know who you are, sir, but I am afraid they are still busy. Give me your number again and I'll get a duty officer to ring you, uniform division. They might help. Oh, not a constable or a sergeant? Okay sir, I'll get a senior officer to ring. Thank you sir."

Thirty minutes later. Inspector Poole. I told him of my situation, and of my appointment as biographer to Estelle's father. He listened intently, and was very helpful, sympathetic even. A gentleman, but with a certain steel in his voice.

"What you tell me is not unusual. Many suicides who commit the act away from home do not leave a note. I do not remember the case myself, I was not at this station then, but this is a very stable station, and it is possible that a P.C. or a sergeant may still be here who worked on the case. We have no records. Why not try the Coroner's Court? They should help." I thanked him. He was kind, and he never flinched when I told him that it was not Fiszel's intention to try to reopen the case, just my own inquisitiveness that demanded the facts.

I rang the Coroner. St. Pancras. Mister Lovegrove.

"Yes sir, we keep those sort of records for 18 years. There may be a transcript of the case as well as an audio tape." Brilliant!

"Can I get to see it?"

"We don't have it here sir. You have to find out if records have it?" Oh, God!

"Give me your number. I'll see if I can help".

One hour later. Telephone.

"Lovegrove here, Coroner's office. I have found the case number. Hearing, 10 October 1977. Case 271, of 1977. I'll give you records' telephone number."

I thanked him profusely. It was a different number than the one given to me by the police telephonist.

"Records, how may I help you?"

I told her my problem; how Mr. Lovegrove had recommended that I ring her.

"I am afraid that you have the wrong office, sir. You will need...."

I rang the alternative number she gave me.

"Coroner's records, Miss Humphrey speaking. May I help you?"

She was sympathetic and helpful. She sounded a lovely lady, gave permission to use her name, and promised to ring me back. I gave her my number.

The telephone, one hour later. Thursday evening, late. "I have found what you need, Mr. Nathan." Success!

"Can I see the transcript?" I enquired.

"I am afraid that that is not possible without the Coroner's office being in attendance. What I can do is to send the papers over to St. Pancras and Mr. Lovegrove will then be able to grant you permission. I hope you find what you are looking for. I'll send the papers right away, first class. They usually get there overnight."
Friday 7 May!
"This is Guy Nathan," after the phone rang for seven minutes.
"I have arranged with records for them to send some papers over to Mr. Lovegrove which he may allow me to inspect this afternoon. I spoke to him yesterday."
"One moment sir." Wait. Five minutes.
"Hello, Mr. Nathan. Mr. Lovegrove is out and will be for the rest of the day. I'll check on his desk to see if the papers are there. What is it all about? Do you have the reference number?"
I gave him the number he wanted. Please. More waiting.
"Hello, Mr. Nathan. There doesn't appear to be anything on his desk. Ring him Monday."
Monday, 10 May. So near. Telephone Lovegrove!
No answer. Five minutes. Then my telephone rings.
"Lovegrove here, Coroner's office, St. Pancras. I have the papers you need to see. If you wish to come up here, I can allow you a peek." Bless him!
"Can I take notes?"
"Hmm, I think that should be okay."
"What about taking a copy of the statements?"
"I'm not sure about that. See when you come in. Tuesday you say. About three. That's fine, I'll be there then."
Tuesday 11 May, arrive Camley Street, exactly three p.m.
I enter the office. About 40 feet square. Four desks. Three people. Mr. Lovegrove, another Coroner's officer and a lady, about thirty,

laughing. Much gaiety in the office of doom. Next door, the mortuary.

"If you wish to sit at that vacant desk, I'll fetch the papers."

They are still making jokes. The atmosphere is relaxed and the people helpful. Light a cigarette.

The first paper is almost illegible, not only from age but because it is written in long hand by the Coroner. He is a Doctor Chambers. It records an interview with Biero Bolognesi at seven p.m. on the night of the 'accident'. Mr. Lovegrove helps me decipher some of the illegible scrawl. What Biero says is contradictory, but it is easy to make a mountain from a molehill! Little things. She took lots of pills. She had no pills. She was depressed, but happy? I telephoned her at 10.30 to 11, but there was no reply. We split up because she said I did not take her out often enough.

Not a great deal to go on. More statements in the file, all typewritten. I have now read through all the statements. If I were looking to reopen the case, I certainly would be trying to find the train driver, whose statement for evidence was the only one considered when the jury came to their verdict. I took notes.

"What about the copies, Mr. Lovegrove?"

"I've done a set for you. If you require anything else, you can have copies of these, too."

"This one, the coroner's report, and this one, the conclusion and this one. What on earth is this doing in the file? Who sent it? Did she have it in her bag? Or was it sent to the coroner after her death?"

A love poem by a strange name! A male! To Estelle? A lover?

At my next interview with Fiszel and Mary, in his home, I posed the question of the poem, and who is Dave Kwiatskowski?

The poem is written by a friend of Larry. No knowledge of any affair between Estelle and this man exists. Mary shakes her head.

Fiszel knows nothing. But there was a lover, and it wasn't Dave Kwiatkowski. I find out that Estelle left Biero and started an affair with a young man who was working as a jeweller, but who wished to return to Israel where he was a soldier. He promised Estelle that if she came with him he would not rejoin the army. The man went. Estelle followed. The lover rejoined the army. Estelle returned to Essex to live with her parents for two weeks, before giving her marriage another chance, after much persuasion from Biero. Where does the poem writer fit in?

Then there are the questions with regard to the evidence contained in the coroner's notes and statements. Why was Biero so intent on starting again? He had no regard for Estelle. Was it that well-known Italian pride? That Sicilian machismo? His connections were probably questionable. He was known to be armed at all times.

Have you ever read or seen something that felt horribly affected by what is there before you? That, dear reader, is how I feel about these events. Estelle was supposedly at her happiest when Biero rang to persuade her to go to an interview for a job. So excited was she that she rang her mother in the morning to tell her of her forthcoming meeting at Swiss Cottage with her husband.

How, in the space of a couple of hours, did she find the courage and the strength to stand in front of a moving underground train? Why, when every time previously she felt so depressed she took an overdose of pills, or in one case cut her wrists, did she on this occasion not call for help?

It just rankles, as an investigative biographer, that I am not able to continue this investigation.

Perhaps, when you read the ensuing papers, reprinted from the files of the coroner, you may form you own conclusions.

The following pages contain photocopies of the documents found in the coroner's file, 16 years after the hearing. I present them without further comment for you to decide whether there could be any doubt about Estelle Bolognesi's death.

BOROUGH OF: St Pancras

CORONER'S OFFICER'S REPORT CONCERNING DEATH

Name: Estella BOLOGNESI
Flat 2,Boundary House, Turner Rd
QueensburympEdgware Middx
Age: 28yrs(1.5.1949 Mile End)

Wife of Biero BOLOGNESI
Occupation: a Retail Manager

Time, Date and   1.25pm
Place of death: 9.9.1977
St.Pancras Public Mortuary,Camley St N.W1

Previous History (operations-accidents-illness) The deceased was a married woman. She had been Seperated from her husband for the past 9mths. Two weeks ago they had been reconciled and she had returned to her home, the husband states although she was depressed she was happy at the thought and arrangements for the future.
No Ops in the past. 10 yrs ago had suffered head injuries in R.T.Acc. No serious injury as a result. General Mental health following the accident had been poor, she had suffered from depression and had been a patient in Goodmayes Hospital and Northbury Hospital. Xmas 1975 had taken and overdose of Tofranil & Tuinol Recently just prior to returning to her husband had taken an overdose.
The family and husband feels that the past overdoses she took were not a serious History of present condition: attempt to end her life, mainly because she had always either telephoned a relative or wrote a letter prior to taking any tablets.
No recent statement of intention to family or friends. Last seen alive by husband 7.50am on 9th Sept when he left arrangements had been made to a job interview, at 4 pm that day.

On Friday 9th September 1977 at about 12.50pm at Swiss Cottage Underground Station a Northbound Bakerloo Line Train was in the tunnel, drawing into the station , when the driver states he saw the deceased person jump in front of the train , from the alcove situated within the tunnel. The only witness is the train driver no other person can witness the deceased entering the tunnel from the station or platform. The train was stopped and the body was recovered from beneath the train by ambulance and Police, obviously dead. The body was conveyed to St Pancras Public Mortuary , Camley Street, N.W.1 where at 1.25pm Dr DALE, Deputy Coroner , was informed and satisfied that the body was dead.

Registered Medical Practitioner attending last illness: Dr SCOTT

Hospital attended, if any: Goodmayes Hospital, Northbury,Middx

N.H.S. Doctor: Dr SCOTT   Does he wish to attend P.M.-Yes/No

Date and time reporter to Officer: 9.9.1977 1.25pm   to Coroner: 9.9.1977 1.25pm
                          by: Pc 152LT TREGUNNO   by: Pc Brown

Was life insured?-Yes/No   Office: Amount:

Was a pension in payment?-Yes/No   War Disablement
                                        Industrial
                                        Retirement

Blame or negligence is alleged by: None Alleged

Is death reportable?-Yes/No   To: Home Office
                                   Authority otherwise

Name and adddress of Registrar: St Pancras Town Hall   Burial
                                                                  Cremation

POST-MORTEM EXAMINATION

...me	Estella Bolognesi	Apparent Age	28 yrs.
At	St. Pancras Mortuary	Date	12.9.77
Identified by	P.C. Brown, Coroner's Officer		

External Examination

Nourishment and Height .. — A well nourished female, 5'3" in height.

Marks of Violence, of Identification, e.g. tattoo marks, old scars, etc. .. .. — There were the following external injuries: The lower part of thorax and upper part of the abdomen were grossly injured with complete exposure of the abdominal wall back to the spine. There were multiple sternal chest injuries, lacerations and bruises and numerous grease marks present over the face and thighs. There were bilateral fractures to both humeri and there were multiple grazes and bruises present on both legs.

Histology; Bacteriology; Toxicology

Time of Death .. .. — 1.25 p.m. 9.9.77

Time of Exam. .. .. — 12.9.77

Internal Examination

Skull .. .. — No fracture.

Brain, Meninges, etc. .. — The brain and meninges appeared normal.

Mouth, Tongue, Oesophagus Larynx, Trachea, Lungs and Pleuræ .. .. .. — The neck showed a little bruising present particularly on the left side. There were multiple rib fractures and severance of the aorta. The lungs showed bilateral bruising.

Weight of R. Lung .. ..

Weight of L. Lung .. ..

Pericardium, Heart and Blood Vessels .. ..

Weight of Heart .. ..

Size of Aorta .. ..

Stomach and Contents .. — In the abdominal cavity there were multiple visceral injuries particularly to the liver and spleen.

Peritoneum, Intestines and Mesenteric Glands .. — No evidence of natural disease was found.

Liver and Gall Bladder ..

Spleen .. .. ..

Kidneys and Ureters ..

Bladder and Urine .. ..

Generative Organs .. ..

Are all other organs healthy?

Did death arise from natural causes? .. .. .. — NO. The injuries are consistent with being caused by a train.

Cause of Death

I

Disease or condition directly leading to death .. .. .. — a. MULTIPLE INJURIES

due to (or as a consequence of)

Antecedent causes. Morbid conditions, if any, giving rise to the above cause stating the underlying condition last. — b. _____ *due to (or as a consequence of)*

c. _____

II

Other significant conditions, contributing to the death, but not related to the disease or condition causing it. — _____

RB19723

Signed _____ PETER VANEZIS M.B., Ch.B., D.M.J. (PATH).

STATEMENT OF WITNESS
(C.J. Act, 1967, ss. 2,9; M.C. Rules, 1968, r. 58)

Statement of .... Geoffrey Denis Tregunno

Age of Witness (if over 21 enter "over 21") ..... Over 21

Occupation of Witness .... Police Constable 152 LT

Address and Telephone Number .... British Transport Police

.... 110 Westminster Bridge Road

.... Lond n S.E.1.

This statement, consisting of   pages each signed by me, is true to the best of my knowledge and belief and I make it knowing that, if it is tendered in evidence, I shall be liable to prosecution if I have wilfully stated in it anything which I know to be false or do not believe to be true.

Dated the 13th day of September   19 77

Signed ..G.D...Tregunno........................

Signature witnessed by ....

On Friday 9 September 1977 I was performing uniform mobile patrol in X Ray 53 with Police Constable LUCKETT. At 1300 hours (1.00pm) as a result of a radio message I attended Swiss Cottage London Transport Station arriving at 1315 (1.15 pm) I went to the northbound Bakerloo line platform where I saw train set No. 153 stationary in the platform, the motormans cab was approximately five yards from the headwall. I went to the rear of the train and saw that the crew of ambulance number F.2162X had removed a body from the track and placed it on a stretcher. I noticed that the platform was dry well lit and clear of all obstruction. The body was taken, by ambulance to St Pancreas Mortuary where at 1335 life was pronounced extinct by Dr. Dale. On searching the handbag found by the body I found a medical certificate for depression in the name of Estelle Bolognesi, of flat 2 Boundary House Turner Road Queensbury Middlesex. The next of kin was eventually informed later that day by Metropolitan

Signed G.D. Tregunno........................   Signature witnessed by ....

BRITISH TRANSPORT POLICE

BR. 7482/1

Continuation of statement of .... Geoffrey Denis Tregunno ....

Police. On Saturday 10 September 1977 I attended St Pancreas

Matuary where at 0950 hours the husband Mr Biero Bolognesi,

of the same address as Estella, identified the property as that

belonging to the deceased. At 1005 the property was restored

to Mr B Bolognesi.

Signed   G.D. Tregunno
.... *Signature Witnessed by* ....

STATEMENT OF WITNESS
(C.J. Act, 1967, ss. 2,9; M.C. Rules, 1968, r. 58)

Statement of .... Richard Denning Humphreys

Age of Witness (if over 21 enter "over 21") ...... Over 21

Occupation of Witness .... Motorman

Address and Telephone Number .... 42 William Saville House

.... Denmark Road Queens Park NW6

This statement, consisting of   pages each signed by me, is true to the best of my knowledge and belief and I make it knowing that, if it is tendered in evidence, I shall be liable to prosecution if I have wilfully stated in it anything which I know to be false or do not believe to be true.

Dated the   10th day of   September   1977

Signed ..... R.D. Humphreys

Signature witnessed by .... J. Morrissey ADS

On Friday 10th September 1977 I was the motorman in charge of

Northbound Bakerloo line train set No. 153, a 7 car train the 1231

hours ex Elephant and Castle to Wembley due at Swiss Cottage at

12.40 hours running to time. As I was approaching the platform

having already made an initial application of the brakes with

the train travelling about 30 miles per hour when suddenly I saw the

form of a person in the shadows a few feet into the tunnel mouth.

I noticed he was moving very fast from right to left in front of

me as if the person had run or jumped. I saw legs and arms moving

rapidly. My train was only about 6 feet from the person when I fir-

st saw it I made an emergency application of the train brakes but

the person disappeared from my view the train coming to a halt

some 5 cars into the platform (250 feet into the platform) My train

when stopped was some 150 feet (3 car lengths) from the normal

stopping point. I secured my train and summoned the assistance of

Signed .... R.D. Humphreys ....   Signature witnessed by .... J Morrissey ADS

Continuation of statement of .... Richard Denning Humphreys

station staff. An Indpector came and I walked with him back to the
tunnel mouth area by use of hand lamps I saw the leg of the person
between the coupling between the 5th and 6th car of the train
(from front) I would say the person had been dragged some 10/12 feet
The Station Inspector got down onto the track and checked the
person. An attempt was made to take the person out between the
couplings but failed. I was then told to allow my train to move
forward slowly until the rear of the train was clear of the person
on the train. This I did. Train was then taken out of service.

Signed .... R.D. Humphreys .... *Signature Witnessed by* .... J Morrissey A.

STATEMENT OF WITNESS
(C.J. Act, 1967, ss. 2,9; M.C. Rules, 1968, r. 58)

Statement of .... Trevor James Rycroft ....

Age of Witness (if over 21 enter "over 21") .. Over 21 ....

Occupation of Witness .... Station Inspector ....

Address and Telephone Number .... CO Finchley Road LT Station ....
.... 450 8622 ....

This statement, consisting of   pages each signed by me, is true to the best of my knowledge
and belief and I make it knowing that, if it is tendered in evidence, I shall be liable to prosecution if
I have wilfully stated in it anything which I know to be false or do not believe to be true.

Dated the   10th day of   September   1977

Signed T. J. Rycroft ....

Signature witnessed by   J Mahoney TDC ....

States I am employed by the London Transport Executive as a Station

Inspector and have been so employed for eight years.

On Friday 9th September 1977 I was the Station Inspector on duty

at Finchley Road Station. At about 1250 pm on information recieved

I went to Swiss Cottage Station. On my arrival at about 12.55 am

I went to the Northbound Bakerloo line platform and there I saw

train Set No.153 stationary about five cars into the platform. I

spoke to the driver Mr Humphreys and he said to me "I think I have

hit someone in the tunnel. I started to walk towards the rear of

the train and was met by Station Foreman Maynard. We both then

walked back and looked under coupling between the fifth and sixth

car. I saw what I though were a pair of feet. I then got down

into the pit and with the aid of cluster lights I could see the

lower part of a body. It was lying between the right hand running

rail and the negative rail. I could not see any other part of

Signed   T.J. Rycroft ....   Signature witnessed by   J Mahoney TDC ....

Continuation of statement of .... Trevor James Rycroft.

the body and it was clear of the train. I then had the train
...moved forward clear of the body. It was then that I saw what
...appeared to be flesh and a hand about 10 feet in the tunnel
...inbetween the right hand running rail and positive rail. I then
...had the traction current discharged at about 1.07 pm. As this was
...done the ambulance crew arrived. They then together with the Stati
...Foreman Maynard picked up the body and took it away. I took no
...further part in the incident. I could not say for certain if the
...body was male of female but it was wearing blue jeans.

STATEMENT OF WITNESS
(C.J. Act, 1967, ss. 2,9; M.C. Rules, 1968, r. 58)

Statement of .... Robert James Ellyat ....

Age of Witness (if over 21 enter "over 21") ....Over...21..

Occupation of Witness .... Ambulance Man ....

Address and Telephone Number .... C/O Ambulance Depot ....

.... Cressy Road NW3 ....

.... 485 2562 ....

This statement, consisting of   pages each signed by me, is true to the best of my knowledge and belief and I make it knowing that, if it is tendered in evidence, I shall be liable to prosecution if I have wilfully stated in it anything which I know to be false or do not believe to be true.

Dated the   10th day of   September   19 77

Signed ....RJ..Ellyat..........................

Signature witnessed by ...J Mahoney TDC

States I am employed by the London Ambulance Service as an

Ambulance man and have been so emp1 yed for eleven months. On

Friday 9th September 1977 on information recieved I attended with my

colleagur Mr Cohen at Swiss Cottage Station at 1.09 pm in ambulance

No. 2167. On my arrival I went to the Northbound Bakerloo line

platform and there I saw a train stationary in the platform. I

walked down the platform to the rear of the train and there about

6 feet from the back of the train by the tunnel mouth I saw part of

the body (THE LOWER PART OF THE TORSO) lying with his feet facing

north inbetween the tight hand running rail and the negative rail.

I then went down onto the track and walked into the tunnel to

try and find the other piece of the torso. We found it about

10/12 feet inside the tunnel with his head facing south and it was

inbetween the right hand running rail and the negative rail. I

went back to the platform and obtained a stretcher and returned to

Signed .....R.J..Ellyat............................   Signature witnessed by ....J Mahoney TDC........

Continuation of statement of .... Robert James Ellyat ....

the tunnel and picked up the upper part of the torso and then the

lower part. There were intestines and I put them in a plastic

bag and placed them on the stretcher. Due to the state of the

body we informed our control that we would be taking it to

St Pancreas Mortuary. On our arrival we placed the body in the

care of Doctor Dale. I could tell the body was female wearing

blue denim jeans, tights, I think she was wearing a black coat.

Signed ....R.J. Ellyat........................   Signature Witnessed by .... J Mahoney ...

STATEMENT OF WITNESS
(C.J. Act, 1967, ss. 2,9; M.C. Rules, 1968, r. 58)

Statement of ..... Kenneth Maynard

Age of Witness (if over 21 enter "over 21") ..... Over 21

Occupation of Witness ..... Station Foreman

Address and Telephone Number ..... C/O Swiss Cottage LT Station

This statement, consisting of   pages each signed by me, is true to the best of my knowledge and belief and I make it knowing that, if it is tendered in evidence, I shall be liable to prosecution if I have wilfully stated in it anything which I know to be false or do not believe to be true.

Dated the   10th   day of   September   1977

Signed ..... K Maynard

Signature witnessed by ..... J Mahoney TDC

States I am employed by the London Transport Executive as a Station Foreman and have been so employed for nine years. On Friday 9th September 1977 I was the Station Foreman on duty at Swiss Cottage Station. At about 12.50 pm I heard the train whistle sound downstairs. I went down to see what the trouble was and on my arrival I saw on the Northbound Bakerloo line platform train set No. 153 stationary about five cars into the platform. I walked towards the motormans cab and the motorman got out and said to me "I think I've got someone under the train at the back" I then looked under the train with the aid of a lamp and I saw under the coupling of the fifth and sixth cars a pair of legs with blue jeans on. A short while afterwards after I had informed the line controller as to what had happened Station Inspector Rycroft arrived. I told him what had taken place. He then got down onto the track and looked under the train with the aid of cluster lights and then informed me that

Signed ..... K Maynard   Signature witnessed by ..... J Mahoney TDC

Continuation of statement of .... Kenneth Maynard

the body was in two parts. Mr Roycroft then had the

train moved forward clear of the body and it was then that I saw

first the lower half of the body lying between the right hand

running rail and the negative rail with the feet facing north and

I also saw about 10 feet in the tunnel the upper part of the body

again lying in between the right hand running rail and the negative

rail. Station Inspector Rycroft then had the current discharged

at 1.07 pm and at this stage the ambulance crew arrived. I

then assisted the ambulance crew in getting the body onto the

stretcher. I saw that the body was that of a female aged about

30 years with brown hair. I then took no further part in the

incident.

Signed .... K Maynard .... Signature Witnessed by .... J Mahoney TDC

STATEMENT OF WITNESS
(C.J. Act, 1967, ss. 2,9; M.C. Rules, 1968, r. 58)

Statement of ..... Diamond Suwaris .....

Age of Witness (if over 21 enter "over 21") ..... Over 21 .....

Occupation of Witness ..... Guard 2660 Queens Park .....

Address and Telephone Number ..... 23 Frith House .....

..... Frampton Street NW8 .....

This statement, consisting of ..... pages each signed by me, is true to the best of my knowledge and belief and I make it knowing that, if it is tendered in evidence, I shall be liable to prosecution if I have wilfully stated in it anything which I know to be false or do not believe to be true.

Dated the 10th day of September 19 77

Signed ..Diamond Suwaris..

Signature witnessed by ..J. Morrissey. ADS

On Friday 10th September 1977 I was the guard in charge of Northbound Bakerloo line train set No153 the 1231 ex Elephant and Castle to Wembley due at Swiss Cottage at 1249 hours running to time. This was a 7 car train. My Motorman made an emergency stop at Swiss Cottage the train coming to a halt ½ way into the platform. I could see this from my guards instrument. I was informed by my motorman of what had happened. I checked the rear of my train and walked forward and assisted in getting all passengers off the train. I did not see or did not become involved in any way with the person under the train. The train was taken out of service.

Signed Diamond Suwaris   *Signature witnessed by* J Morrissey ADS

"THE PURPOSE OF MY LIFE"

THE PURPOSE OF MY LIFE... IS YOU MY LOVE
YOU ARE WARM...... NO STRANGER
SO GLAD GOD PUT YOU ON EARTH
YOU ARE IN NO DANGER
AND I LOVE YOU, FOR WHAT YOU ARE
SO NATURAL AND SINCERE
MORNING LIGHT, AND WE ARE ALRIGHT
EVERYTHING IS CLEAR

THE PURPOSE OF MY LIFE.... IS YOU MY LOVE
OUR LOVE IS NO GAME
YOU ARE MY STRENGTH... WHEN I FEEL BAD
OUR LOVE HOLD'S NO SHAME
YES MY LOVE, ALL MY WORD'S ARE TRUE
LIKE WHAT I FEEL INSIDE
I BELIEVE IN LOVE.. I BELIEVE IN YOU
SO MUCH HERE INSIDE

YOU ARE THE PURPOSE OF MY LIFE
ONE THAT WILL NEVER DIE
SO GLAD YOUR LOVE IS MINE
YOU WILL NEVER CRY
LET US KISS NOW, ANGEL FACE
SO SWEET THE MAGIC TOUCH
YOU ALWAYS MAKE MY HEARTBEAT RACE
I LOVE YOU.. VERY MUCH .

DAVE KWIATKOWSKI .
AUG 77

CHAPTER 4

1977-1992

The death of Estelle was to have long-term and short-term effects of momentous proportions on Fiszel and his family. Strangely, it was Fiszel himself who seemed to have suffered the most, and equally surprisingly Yetta who took the burden upon her own shoulder in the time-worn manner of a Yiddisher mamma. Or so it seemed at the time. Fiszel entered into a deep depression, flamed by his hatred of Biero and that man's cavalier behaviour in observing the 'shiva' for only two days before he disappeared out of the family's life, virtually forever. The only knowledge that Fiszel has of Biero's existence to this day is a series of letters sent by Barclaycard just a few months later, enquiring about the use of his wife's credit card in Italy. Estelle's husband left the bereft home of Maralyn, where the family sat on their low stools for the customary period of one week, never to appear again. The funeral was itself a traumatic experience, for Estelle had lost touch with the Jewish faith and the elders of the synagogue were reluctant to bury a suicide on their sacred grounds, which again is a traditional attitude. Eventually Fiszel paid the synagogue who, reluctantly and without ceremony, buried the girl's remains in a grave some way from those who had died in more normal circumstances.

Unable to work on, Fiszel entered a period of depression that was to last for six months. Unbelieving of the hand of fate which had selected him once again, he refused to go back to the factory which had been so much a part of his life as well as his main income and ended his working life by literally giving the company to Joan, his partner. The thoughts of Estelle's death, and the manner in which she died, played heavily on his mind, but somehow, calling on that inherent strength that had served him so well during those dark days of the Second World War, he slowly accepted that his eldest daughter was gone forever. Yetta, in the meantime, and perhaps for the first time in their lives, offered sympathy and understanding, and his bed back to him, to comfort her distressed husband.

She was not to know that in summoning upon a strength that was alien to her character and personality, she was starting on the trail that would lead to an early and painful death.

In March of the following year, 1978, unable to continue living at their home, the family, with the exception of Larry, moved down to the Essex coast, freeing themselves of the memories and the suffering that pervaded their house. It was then that Fiszel, this time with Mary and Roy Miller, commenced a partnership that was to become a long and impregnable friendship. Slowly Fiszel returned to normality, and the new house brought with it a new beginning.

Yetta settled into her new home, and life, for just a few months, was kind to her, for outwardly she appeared to be coping and managing the household and living with the death of her daughter with dignity and resolve. But it was a facade

In 1979 a minor argument with Suzanne, one which any mother can have with a daughter, caused her to snap and she rushed upstairs to a window and this time succeeded in throwing herself from the first floor, landing on the roof of the kitchen, crashing through onto her back. Suzanne immediately called for an ambulance, and Yetta was transferred to Rochford Hospital, where she was diagnosed as having endogenous depression, while her physical injuries were somewhat miraculously minor. She had a broken leg, some abrasions and severe bruising on all parts of her body. After a period of treatment, she was transferred to the very hospital in which Larry remains, Runwell. (I am pleased to report that Larry is recovering from his own trauma at the time of writing and is now allowed home for weekends, and will soon, hopefully, be discharged.) At the mental institute Yetta received a series of electro-convulsion therapy shocks, the last of which caused her heart to fail. A supreme effort on behalf of the hospital staff somehow revived her, but she was never to be the same again. After three months she was to return home, again to adopt the dignified manner that she had so successfully shown previously, but her physical condition had deteriorated and her inner strength was in decline.

It was in early 1980 that another problem to rock the growing stability of the family was to occur again. This time it was Suzanne who presented her mother and father with a boy friend who was unacceptable, and one whom she had decided to marry. The boy, Rory, was from a strict Catholic household, and with much experience Fiszel once again advised his offspring not to marry. It was at this time that Maralyn gave birth to a daughter on 16 June, 1978 named Emma, after her dead sister. In the Jewish faith, an English name bearing the same initial letter invariably bears an identical name in Hebrew. Hence Emma can be construed as being in memory of Estelle. Learning from past experiences, Fiszel this time went to the registry office wedding, horribly aware of the failed marriage of his eldest daughter, and the difficulties that the middle daughter Maralyn was having with her husband, Chas.

In August 1980, Suzanne married her man, but not before an aunt of the groom had visited to advise that Rory had undergone a brain tumour operation which had left him with what she termed a personality defect. She pleaded with Fiszel to stop the marriage taking place, but he was powerless to do so. It would seen that the marriage had little chance of surviving from the beginning because Rory's mother also vociferously objected to the union. While Fiszel and Yetta accepted the situation, perhaps in a most pragmatic way, Rory's mother was never to agree to the marriage and was to spend her days in obsessive objection, until finally her power over her son was to succeed in breaking the two of them up. It was significant also that Chas did not attend the wedding, held in the family home, while Maralyn and her young baby did so.

Shortly after this event, Yetta was to re-enter Runwell and Rochford as she was now diagnosed as having diabetes and emphysema, a wasting of body tissue usually affecting the lungs, which at the time was containable, but not curable.

Yetta was on a downward slide, and began to age alarmingly, her hair turning prematurely grey, and her body becoming emaciated and frail. Fiszel and Mary took her to Majorca, and then to Israel, in the hope that the warm Mediterranean sun coupled with meeting some of his old colleagues, even his cousins who had so mercilessly evicted him from their home after his final release to Zdunska-Wola in 1945, would help. But nothing could halt the poor woman's incurable illnesses and deteriorating mental state, not even the birth of a second child to Maralyn, this time a boy called Elliott, born on 26 January 1981. Even this happy event was to turn sour, for Maralyn was convinced that the boy had a physical defect, and for six weeks she pleaded and begged the doctors to closely examine him. It would appear that he was unable to keep his food down, and a mother knows, doesn't she? Driving herself relentlessly, Maralyn suffered a nervous breakdown when she learned that her new offspring had Pylorich Stinosis, which meant an immediate life-saving operation. The boy survived. His mother broke down and attempted suicide by way of an overdose of sleeping pills and was duly admitted to Goodmayes hospital. This was to be the first of a series of attempted suicides and a series of admittances to mental hospitals.

In 1982 Larry completed the set by marrying outside of his religion. It was also at this time that Yetta suffered a heart attack and was fitted with a pacemaker. She was on borrowed time. For two further years she was to be admitted to various hospitals, until she became disorientated from the effects of the medicines and the pills and the treatment, which was to include further bouts of E.C.T.

With Mary at her bedside, and with her last words 'Look after Phil for me', the brave and wonderful mother who had endured untold hardships and derived so little satisfaction from this life, passed away. It was December 1984. Yetta was only 61 years of age. She had lived long enough to see another two grandchildren born; one to Larry and his wife Shirley, a boy David, on 20 June, and another to Suzanne and Rory, a daughter Natalie, on 26 April.

This latest addition to the Lisner flock became the spur that Rory's mother needed to accelerate her continuing objections to her son's union and she brought unbearable pressure on her young and timid daughter-in-law, who followed what was becoming a trend by having a semi-breakdown. This collapse provided the vindictive and unforgiving woman with the weapon she needed to persuade the Social Services that Suzanne was not a fit mother. Her efforts were eventually rewarded when Suzanne gave birth to her second child, a son Lawrence, in April 1987. Starved now of the affections of her weak husband, apparently almost totally under the influence of his mother, Suzanne continued to be distressed and found herself incapable of giving the love that was needed to her newborn child. Fiszel tried to help, and after the baby and mother had been allowed home from hospital, he visited in order to see his grandson. But

Suzanne could not face visitors of any kind, including her own father, and Fiszel failed to see the boy. For two months he tried everything in his power, persuasion, telephone calls, messages etc., but to no avail. While everything possible was being done for Suzanne by her close friends, sister and father, the now notorious mother-in-law was warning the Social Services of assumed, potential danger to her grandchildren. Finally, she applied for a court order, which was granted with the backing of that body of well-meaning people. Immediately afterwards, three policeman and a social worker hammered alarmingly on Suzanne's front door, demanding entry. This in the middle of the night, Gestapo style!

Rory had left his wife, oblivious of her personal distress, and allowed his mother to take the reins. The social worker dragged the now three-year-old Natalie and the new-born Lawrence away. For two months thereafter, Larry accompanied Suzanne for fortnightly visits, until the youngest was fostered out and the girl placed under the guardianship of her grandmother. Fiszel was denied this facility, although the law of Great Britain today would give him these rights.

The whereabouts of Lawrence are to this day unknown to Fiszel, and he has never laid eyes on his grandson.

As far as the family is aware, Natalie lives relatively comfortably with her guardian (grandmother), and is being brought up in the faith of the woman's choice.

I asked why Lawrence was not taken in by his grandmother. It would appear that after Rory left Suzanne she took a lover and there is doubt about the baby's parentage, although Suzanne insists to this day that the baby is of her husband, who visited frequently during their separation. The mother was in no doubt that the baby is not of her blood, and has made no request to the court for guardianship.

These events resulted in a complete nervous breakdown for Suzanne, but she has always refused hospital admission and on many occasions the drugs that her medical advisers prescribed. To this day Suzanne is disturbed and timid, fearful of any type of institution or collective organisation. I have tried to interview her and have even made an appointment, but she failed to turn up. I have only the utmost sympathy for her, and hope that Fiszel sees the day when she is fully recovered and in charge of her own destiny. Most of all I hope that she achieves a quality of life that has, by poor decision and uncompromising relatives, been denied her in the past.

Maralyn, in the interim, has also suffered great deprivation and duress. Her marriage foundered in 1989. In 1985 she had another daughter, Yvette, but the birth left her again with a deep post-natal depression, and she has had many breakdowns and admissions to a number of hospitals, nearly all dealing with problems of the mind. Following one such admittance, in July 1991, she returned home to find that the locks on the doors of her house had been changed and the children gone. They are now divorced and she resides with a close male friend to whom she has given another daughter, Jessica. Remarkably, like her mother Yetta before her, she has had three girls and one boy!

Larry languishes in Runwell Hospital, estranged from Shirley, who is planning divorce. She bore him a second son, Simon, in 1986, and father and sons are for the first time separated. Of all of Fiszel's offspring, Larry is the one with most control and vivid memories of the family's past, and it is tragic to see him as his mother and sisters before him, a patient in a mental institution. He is receiving counselling, and I do believe that he will recover. He is a good-looking young man who will, as the hurt subsides, find a new life, and I expressed surprise that he should have given way to the strain of the break up of his marriage.

I am appalled at his reason. Not appalled at its substance, but at the insensitivity of his wife. Her lover is called Wolfgang! Of all the heartbreak that Larry has had to witness, of all the trauma to which he has been privy, nothing has affected him more than to know that his wife is associating with a German. The irony is beyond comprehension and understanding. Shirley left Larry in 1992, and he was coping well with frequent visits to his former home and unlimited access to his children. He still has the access, but when he discovered the nationality of his wife's lover it became too much.

Finally, that leaves Fiszel. Since Yetta's death, he has lived at their family home, Mary and Roy having unselfishly sold their house to move in with him and take care of him. He too has suffered personal trauma to continue the trend of his miserable and deprived life, and that of his children.

His back is still troublesome and it appears that he will never be without his nightmares, which continue to invade his being and his soul.

On a more pragmatic front, the nightmare of the mistake made by the clerk in Bergen-Belsen in 1946 has come back to haunt him in a number of ways.

In 1991 he applied for the old-age pension and was requested to produce a birth certificate. He subsequently wrote to the Polish authorities, or more precisely Maralyn wrote for him, and remarkably they found his original registration. Remarkable because, way back in those dark days, half the population, particularly the Jewish people, failed to register their new offspring. When he received the copy of the original certificate it showed, understandably, his correct date of birth. He had lived until the evening of his life in the belief that he was four years younger than he otherwise knew. Incredibly, the British Government have refused to pay the full amount due of back-pay and have offered just one extra year. The ramifications of this discovery have had a more severe effect on his bank loan and insurance policies. On admitting his folly to his bank manager the terms of his remaining debt on his house have been called into question, as he would have no mortgage protection policy or life policy to support this loan. At one point he was threatened with eviction, and it was only pressure brought by various groups upon the insurance company that persuaded them to sustain his policy by way of increased monthly payment. This has placed enormous financial strain upon him, as he is only able to attend the markets for a couple of days each week, and his combined income, particularly during the recent recessionary times, just about keeps his head above water.

He suffered too when he had an accident while driving home from one of his days at the market. On Christmas Eve 1990 the brakes failed as he swerved to avoid contact with three cars stationed at a red light junction. He hit the wall of a nearby building, and bouncing off, rendered himself and Mary, who was with him, unconscious. His recovery was slow and financially debilitating, and it is only his courage, about which I have written so often in this biography, that has enabled him once again to face adversity.

It may be that the reader will think that Fiszel is a beaten old man, dispirited by the tragic and traumatic events of his life. But this is not so. He laughs easily and is a joy to be with, demonstrating unqualified affection and enthusiasm for everyone he meets. People are immediately impressed by his charisma and warm humble greetings. I am forced to ask how he does it?

I have made reference to the reasons for what can only be described as the submissions to life of his family, and the cause. I firstly spoke with Maralyn. I found her lethargic, sometimes incomprehensible, and often unable to understand my questions. Perhaps it was the drugs The pills. I really don't know even if she was taking these at the time of our meeting in May 1993. I wanted a reaction, but received none. She states that her doctors have often mentioned hereditary genetic causes, but not all of them. Some think that her breakdowns and submissions to pressure are a result of her difficult background. Suzanne, as I have previously mentioned, will not speak to me after I first met her by accident when she arrived at Fiszel's home during an interview. I can say that she too, at that meeting, was slow and lethargic and not entirely responsive.

Larry has always been more enthusiastic about the book, about life, about his family. In many ways he would appear to be almost the surrogate father; for the one thing that all the children have been in agreement about is their father's absences from the 'mettel' of their lives. Larry asks what might have been if Fiszel had opened up and told them the story of his younger life and got it off his chest in their early days. Until now, they had all only heard snippets, and none of the children knew of the horrendous years and the suffering, the humiliations, the torment. Larry agrees that his father might have had every reason to leave the disappointing bosom of family life. It is only now, in the telling of this story, that he realises what a difficult marriage his parents had.

In summary, I do not believe that there is any single explainable reason for the events in Fiszel's life. Not for his continued suffering. Not for the collapse of his family, the break-up of his children's marriages, the poison arrow of the Maker being continually aimed in his direction. What I do know is that Fiszel Lisner is the most remarkable, brave, tenacious, and deprived human being about whom I have ever written and am likely to write of in the future. Long may he live in peace and comfort, and LOVE. June 1993

The End

At the time of commencing writing, Myer Sworzyinski, Fiszel's friend and saviour in Frankfurt-on-Main, the scallywag who seemed to have invented black marketeering as an art form, was alive. We have heard that he has since passed away. R.I.P.

To our knowledge, Henya, Fiszel's first real love, Chaim, who saved his life when he was strung-up by the Nazis for leaving the camp to find food, and his two cousins, who you will remember escaped the Final Solution to the Lodz ghetto are all still alive. May they enjoy their remaining years in peace and love.

It is also pleasing to write that Larry has been discharged from Runwell Hospital and has started back at work, even finding some common ground with Shirley. Who knows, maybe they'll get back together.

Fiszel & Yetta on their wedding day, July, 1948.

Bendet and his five sisters safely in the USA from
exile in Sweden.

The proud parents with son Larry at his Barmitzvah ,1963.

Estelle, 1969.

Mary Miller with her daughter and the ageing Yetta, 1981.

Fiszel, Yetta, Larry, daughter Suzanne and husband Rory.

Yetta and Fiszel on honeymoon,
Margate,1948.

Fiszel at his market stall, 1992.

Fiszel & his life long friend Bendet, Detroit ,1990.

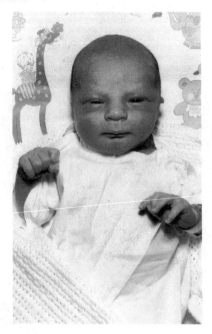

Suzanne's baby Lawrence who Fiszel
has never seen.

Emma, Maralyn's eldest,
named after Aunty Estelle ...

... and as a baby in father Chas's arms,
1980 ...

... and Maralyn.

Fiszel with youngest daughter Suzanne ,1993....

... with son Larry and grandson David ,1992.

Larry's youngest, Simon, 1992.

Mary Miller, 1992.

BRITISH NATIONALITY ACT, 1948.

CERTIFICATE OF NATURALISATION

Whereas　　Fiszel Lisner

has applied to one of Her Majesty's Principal Secretaries of State for a certificate of naturalisation, alleging with respect to　him self the particulars set out below, and has satisfied the Secretary of State that the conditions laid down in the British Nationality Act, 1948, for the grant of a certificate of naturalisation are fulfilled :

Now, therefore, the Secretary of State, in pursuance of the powers conferred upon him by the said Act, grants to the said

Fiszel Lisner

this Certificate of Naturalisation, and declares that upon taking the Oath of Allegiance within the time and in the manner required by the regulations made in that behalf he shall be a citizen of the United Kingdom and Colonies as from the date of this certificate.

In witness whereof I have hereto subscribed my name this　*15.* day of *April* , 19 *55*

HOME OFFICE,
LONDON.

J a Newsam

UNDER SECRETARY OF STATE.

PARTICULARS RELATING TO APPLICANT.

Full Name	Fiszel LISNER.
Address	9, Lyndhurst Court, Churchfields, London, E.18.
Profession or Occupation	Machinist (Ladies' Tailoring).
Place and date of birth	Zdunska-Wola, Poland.　23rd November, 1928.
Nationality	Polish.
Single, married, etc.	Married.
Name of wife or husband	Yetta.
Names and nationalities of parents	Abram Beer Luzer and Ester Laya LISNER (Polish).

Oath of Allegiance

*Insert
Full Name I,* FISZEL LISNER

swear by Almighty God that I will be faithful and bear true allegiance to Her Majesty, Queen Elizabeth the Second, Her Heirs and Successors, according to law.

(Signature)   F. Lisner

Sworn and subscribed this 22 day of April 1955 , before me,

(Signature)   A. M. Plight

Justice of the Peace for A Commissioner for Oaths
A Commissioner for Oaths.

Name and Address
(in Block Capitals)   A. M. Plight

1 COMMERCIAL STREET, E.1.

Unless otherwise indicated hereon, if the Oath of Allegiance is not taken within one calendar month of the date of this Certificate, the Certificate is of no effect.

HOME OFFICE
28 APR 1955
REGISTERED

POLSKA RZECZPOSPOLITA LUDOWA

URZĄD STANU CYWILNEGO w ....Zduńskiej.Woli...........

Województwo ...sieradzkie...............

Nr ...84/5/1926... Zduńska Wola ...., data ...19 stycznia 1926 r.

Odpis zupełny aktu urodzenia

I. DANE DOTYCZĄCE DZIECKA:

1. Nazwisko   L I S N E R   ------------------------

2. Imię (imiona) ...FISZEL ----------- 3. Płeć ...męska ----

4. Data urodzenia   drugiego stycznia,tysiąc dziewięćset dwudziestego czwartego /02.01.1924/ roku ----

5. Miejsce urodzenia   Zduńska Wola ------------------

II. DANE DOTYCZĄCE RODZICÓW:

	Ojciec	Matka
1. Nazwisko	Lisner ---------	Kaszewicz -----
2. Imię (imiona) . .	Luzer ----------	Estera Łaja ---
3. Nazwisko rodowe .	Lisner --------	Kaszewicz -----
4. Data urodzenia .	lat 26 --------	lat 20 --------
5. Miejsce urodzenia.	---------------	---------------
6. Miejsce zamieszkania w chwili urodzenia dziecka	Zduńska Wola --	---------------

III. DANE DOTYCZĄCE OSOBY (ZAKŁADU) ZGŁASZAJĄCEJ URODZENIE:

1. Nazwisko i imię (nazwa zakładu) **Lisner Luzer --------**

2. Miejsce zamieszkania (siedziba zakładu) **Zduńska Wola ---**

IV. UWAGI:

Podpis osoby zgłaszającej
/-/ **Lisner**
KIEROWNIK

Urzędu Stanu Cywilnego

Wzmianki dodatkowe: /-/ **Podpis nieczytelny**

Miejsce
na opłatę
skarbową

Poświadcza się zgodność powyższego odpisu z treścią aktu w księdze urodzeń.

Zduńska Wola, data 1992-04-22

KIEROWNIK
Urzędu Stanu Cywilnego

w. z. Marga Chrzanowska
zastępca

Pu-M-4 zam. 970 WA Olsztyn
PDA SSK ,,Pojezierze" zam 65/89 (215 000) A5

3

PHOTOGRAPH OF HOLDER AND
STAMP OF ISSUING AUTHORITY
PHOTOGRAPHIE DU TITULAIRE
ET CACHET DE L'AUTORITE QUI
DELIVRE LE TITRE

PHOTO... OF
H... FE
...IE DE
TIT...ULAIRE

PHOTO...
TIT...

FINGER-PRINTS OF HOLDER
(if required)
EMPREINTES DIGITALES DU
TITULAIRE
(facultatif)

Signature of Bearer—Signature du Titulaire.

S. Disnea

This document contains 32 pages, exclusive of cover.
Ce titre contient 32 pages, non compris la couverture.

2

Place and date of birth
Lieu et date de naissance } **2 DMSM 23rd NOV. 1928**

Occupation
Profession } ....

Present residence
Résidence actuelle } **LONDON**

*Maiden name and forename(s) of wife
Nom (avant le mariage) et prénom(s)
de l'épouse } ....

*Name and forename(s) of husband
Nom et prénom(s) du mari } ....

DESCRIPTION — SIGNALEMENT

Height
Taille } **5 ft. 6 in.**

Hair
Cheveux } **DARK BROWN**

Colour of eyes
Couleur des yeux } **LIGHT GREEN**

Nose
Nez } **NORMAL**

Shape of face
Forme du visage } **OVAL**

Complexion
Teint } **FAIR**

Special peculiarities
Signes particuliers } **NONE**

CHILDREN — ENFANTS		
Name Nom / Forenames Prénom(s)	Place and date of birth Lieu et date de naissance	Sex Sexe

*Strike out whichever does not apply.
*Biffer la mention inutile.

This document contains 32 pages, exclusive of cover.
Ce titre contient 32 pages, non compris la couverture.

ORDER THESE BOOKS POST & PACKING FREE!

KINNOCK
Dr George Drower
Introduction by the Rt Hon Gerald Kaufman, MP. Special contribution Glenys Kinnock.
Based on interviews with the former Labour leader and his political friends and enemies, this is a remarkable insight into the character and personality of the man who might have been.
Biography/politics
Hardback; 408pp with photographs; £16.99

A MAN DEPRIVED
Fiszel Lisner and Guy Nathan
Extremely harrowing and moving, this is the story of the man who survived the Nazi death camps for longer than anyone - one week short of five years.
Biography/history
Paperback; 208pp; £6.99

THE ANGEL WITHIN
Helen Wade
Introduction by Damon Hill
Humorous and harrowing but ultimately wonderfully uplifting and inspirational, this is the story of the life of a mother of a child with Down's Syndrome.
Biography/sociology
Paperback; 252pp; £6.99

EASTENDERS DON'T CRY
Joe Morgan
Known to his friends as Father Joe and to his enemies as The Godfather, Joe Morgan, former leader of Basildon Council and one of the Labour movement's most active political irritants, tells all in a thoroughly readable account of his life and loves.
Autobiography
Paperback; 180pp; £4.99

THE DEVIL'S DAUGHTER
Christine Hart
Foreword by Colin Wilson
The incredible story of the girl who came to believe she was the daughter of notorious Moors murderer Ian Brady.
Autobiography
Paperback; 282pp; £5.99

BARCELONA TO BEDLAM
Guy Nathan
Foreword by Reg Drury, former News of the World sports reporter.
Highly topical given Tottenham Hotspur's present predicament, this is the true story of Terry Venables and Alan Sugar and of how a marriage seemingly made in Heaven was consummated in Hell.
Sport/business
Paperback; 382pp; £9.95

GEORDIE PASSION
Mark Hannen - Foreword by Peter Beardsley
The captivating chronicle of the author's lifetime devotion to Newcastle United Football Club. From his early years in the late 1960s to the present day, this is a testimony, written from the heart, to a game that incorporates all of life's emotions in a way no other can.
Sport
Hardback; 164pp with photographs; £9.99

BIG JACK
Stan Liversedge.
The life and times of one of the most widely-respected international football managers who guided Ireland to the 94 World Cup finals and the sensational victory over Italy. A fascinating and throughly enjoyable read.
Sport/biography
Hardback; 172pp with photographs; £9.99

LIVING, LOVING, LEARNING
Clarke Jaggard
Published posthumously, after the author's tragic death in a car accident when
he was barely 20, this is a beautiful collection of Clarke Jaggard's poems of
love and life and dreams.
Poetry
Paperback; 24pp; £3.95

THE A-Z OF USES FOR AN UNEMPLOYED PERSON
Miles
A sparkling collection of cartoons by the famous ex-cartoonist several newspapers
and publications.
Humour
Paperback; 28pp; £1.95

LEGACY OF GREED
Alan Wells
In this high-tension, topical story of international intrigue and conspiracy, a
formidable, beautiful diplomat is suspected of sabotaging Anglo-Chinese
negotiations over Hong Kong.
Fiction
Paperback; 348pp; £4.99

These books can be ordered post and packing free. Just send
cash, cheque or postal order to the value of the book(s) to:

The Publishing Corporation UK Ltd,
Haltgate House,
52-54 Hullbridge Road,
South Woodham Ferrers,
Essex CM3 5NH
Tel/fax: 0245 320462

Please allow 28 days for delivery.